I0568520

Abusive People

Healing Your Heart After Emotionally Abusive Relationship

(Effective Methods and Exercises to Recognize Manipulative and Emotionally Abusive People)

Thomas Rouse

Published By **Bella Frost**

Thomas Rouse

All Rights Reserved

Abusive People: Healing Your Heart After Emotionally Abusive Relationship (Effective Methods and Exercises to Recognize Manipulative and Emotionally Abusive People)

ISBN   978-1-998769-78-0

No part of this guidebook shall be reproduced in any form without permission in writing from the publisher except in the case of brief quotations embodied in critical articles or reviews.

Legal & Disclaimer

The information contained in this ebook is not designed to replace or take the place of any form of medicine or professional medical advice. The information in this ebook has been provided for educational & entertainment purposes only.

The information contained in this book has been compiled from sources deemed reliable, and it is accurate to the best of the Author's knowledge; however, the Author cannot guarantee its accuracy and validity and cannot be held liable for any errors or omissions. Changes are periodically made to this book. You must consult your doctor or get professional medical advice before using any of the suggested remedies, techniques, or information in this book.

Upon using the information contained in this book, you agree to hold harmless the Author from and against any damages, costs, and expenses, including any legal fees potentially resulting from the application of any of the information provided by this guide. This disclaimer applies to any damages or injury caused by the use and application, whether directly or indirectly, of any advice or information presented, whether for breach of contract, tort, negligence, personal injury, criminal intent, or under any other cause of action.

You agree to accept all risks of using the information presented inside this book. You need to consult a professional medical practitioner in order to ensure you are both able and healthy enough to participate in this program.

TABLE OF CONTENTS

Chapter 1: What Is Manipulation And

Emotional Abuse?

According to Women's College Hospital, a observe conducted on emotional abuse in 1995 tested approximately 1000 ladies elderly 15 and above. The results showed that a spectacular 36 percentage of women had suffered from emotional abuse even as developing up; roughly 43 percentage had experienced some form of abuse at some stage in their youth and childhood; and around 39 percentage of the women had skilled emotional abuse in their intimate relationships within the past five years. Sadly, the situation has best worsened. Because many human beings do now not take into account emotional abuse a valid shape of abuse, most lack knowledge approximately the difficulty, permitting emotional abuse to amplify at an alarming price.

As we explore this topic extra deeply, we can discuss what precisely constitutes emotional abuse and controlling conduct, and overview a number of the main myths associated with them.

Understanding Emotional Abuse

Broken bones, bruises, open wounds, and swollen eyes are capability symptoms of bodily violence and abuse, and are usually pretty easy to spot. However, there's another kind of abuse that does not leave any bodily tangible or visible marks. The consequences and lasting affects of this form of abuse are potentially greater and extra unfavourable than the aforementioned bodily signs and symptoms. It is the sort of abuse that scars your soul and damages your mind. Yes, we're relating to emotional and psychological abuse.

So what's emotional abuse? Currently, there isn't extensively familiar definition used to accurately describe what emotional abuse is. This is due to the fact emotional abuse is many things, and can take many forms. Emotional abuse can be described as a form of violence routed inside the abuser's need for power and manipulate. Emotional abuse can appear itself at instances inside the shape of verbal abuse. Verbal abuse, verbal bullying, or reviling is a form of abuse in which the abuser says negative and dangerous defining statements about the sufferer, or withholds wonderful verbal and behavioral comments from the victim.

Moreover, victims of manipulative controlling human beings often turn out to be affected by emotional abuse because the abuser will make the most emotions which include guilt, fear, and love to make you do stuff you wouldn't typically do. You may additionally frequently sense tired, or drained when coping with these kinds of humans. You may additionally revel in symptoms akin to post-traumatic strain, as in case you are experiencing intellectual and emotional whiplash. You may additionally begin to second guess your thoughts and moves and turn out to be progressively uncertain of yourself. You can also sense out of balance such as you can not do anything right, or something to delight your abuser. And the cruel fact is -

you can't please your abuser. You might imagine their worrying behavior is motivated by way of love and with the aid of them wanting you to be the pleasant model of your self, while in fact it's miles all approximately manage. They are playing a game that you weren't even aware become being performed.

Frequently, manipulative conduct is expressed thru verbal abuse. Comprised of 1 or more the subsequent actions:

• Expressing anger via the abuser with the victim in the shape of abusive language and slanderous comments.

• Blaming and accusing the sufferer of things they haven't even achieved, or blaming them for the problems faced via the abuser.

• Countering the whole lot the sufferer says.

• Denial by means of the abuser that they may be emotionally abusive with the victim.

• Constantly criticizing and belittling the sufferer.

• Calling the victim irrelevant and abusive names.

• Threatening to depart the sufferer, or remove something important to them.

• Withholding love, care, affection and intimacy from the victim.

• Abusing the sufferer on the premise of sexual discrimination and racism.

• Gas lights, that is twisting the reality and data in a manner that it favors the abuser and portrays the victim as the real culprit.

• Dictating every pass of the sufferer and dominating them.

• Manipulating and exploiting the sufferer on the idea of their weaknesses and manipulating them to obey the abuser at all charges.

If you've got been affected by any of the above behaviors, and the man or woman causing it on you does no longer experience that their moves are wrong; acknowledges their abusive behavior, however does no longer express regret to you; or apologizes to you, but keeps with the abuse, unfortunately you're one of the lots of goals of verbal abuse. Constant publicity to such verbally abusive behavior can result in you affected by the very negative effects of emotional abuse.

Are Psychological Abuse and Emotional Abuse the Same?

Psychological abuse, also called emotional abuse, mental abuse, or mental violence is a kind of abuse wherein you are exposed to a mentally traumatic behavior that causes psychological trauma. The trauma can occur itself in numerous bureaucracy including submit-traumatic pressure sickness, persistent melancholy, extreme tension ailment, conditions associated with self-photograph, cut up persona disorders, and various different intellectual and emotional issues.

Psychological abuse is a broader class of abuse that is produced from emotional abuse, verbal abuse, and controlling manipulative behavior.

While verbal abuse might not usually bring about psychological trauma, mental abuse continually results in some form of psychological trauma. Psychological aggression may be grouped into 3 classes:

• Verbal Aggression: Saying some thing frightening or traumatic.

• Dominant Behavior: Preventing or now not allowing someone to touch his or her cherished ones.

• Jealous Behavior: Accusing your partner of dishonest, being unfaithful, or being disloyal.

If you're being subjected to those behaviors, and it's far affecting your emotional balance and intellectual nicely-being, then you are a victim of psychological abuse. Continuous publicity to verbal and emotional abuse can soon become psychological violence. And when you are often being attacked with abusive remarks and call calling, preserving mental balance beneath those instances is very hard.

With the above in mind, let us attention on some of the myths associated with verbal and emotional abuse.

Myths Related To Emotional Abuse

Several studies have proven that emotionally abused humans suffer from low self-esteem, depression, chronic strain, chronic tension, and can even strive suicide. Unfortunately, there are a few dangerous myths related to emotional abuse in spite of the dangerous results experienced via its sufferers. Below are a number of the maximum common.

Emotional abuse isn't substantial.

Emotional abuse can happen in any type of courting, and it's miles a worldwide problem. And one of the maximum heart-wrenching relationship dynamics wherein this conduct is perpetrated is within the emotional abuse of youngsters.

Verbal abuse isn't a large problem.

Another fantasy shows that verbal abuse isn't a serious difficulty due to the fact words don't motive wounds, however it's miles handiest bodily accidents that depend. However, research have confirmed that merciless and cruel words at once harm your shallowness and self-self belief. When your self confidence shatters, you start devaluing your self, and lack the courage to do or say the things you want to. This therefore damages your intellectual health, and paves the way for the mental situations mentioned above.

Men are chargeable for controlling and disciplining their spouses/partners.

Many cultures and societies are still of the opinion that guys are superior to ladies. Some even agree with that men have the right to manipulate and area their spouses/partners. So, if a husband or boyfriend shouts at his female counterpart, calls her derogatory names, or is inflicting any form of emotional abuse, it is erroneously believed to be k because it's miles his obligation to subject her. Every person, be it a individual has the proper to live their lifestyles their personal way, and their spouses/companions do not have the proper to discipline or manage them.

The sufferer deserved it or become at fault.

Some human beings wrongly trust that if you are stricken by emotional and mental abuse, it is due to the fact you're at fault and you've achieved some thing incorrect and are deserving of being treated this way. Nobody deserves to be abused in any form of way, and there is not anything you probably did or said that made you deserving of emotional abuse. The manner your abuser feels or behaves isn't always your fault. Every grownup is responsible for managing his or her personal feelings. So, if your abuser can't manage their feelings and feelings, and takes their anger out on you rather than venting in the precise way, it's far their fault - no longer yours. There isn't anything you're doing that warrants emotional abuse. Remember this in mind, and don't permit all and sundry convince you otherwise.

Emotional abuse simplest includes yelling and call calling.

Another false impression related to emotional abuse is that it best includes yelling and name calling. Many believe that if your abuser is insulting you in any other manner, or is manipulating you thru threats or fuel lights, then it does not fall beneath the class of emotional or mental abuse. They are incorrect. If you are continuously being belittled by your abuser, dominated, or publicly humiliated - then you are a sufferer of emotional abuse.

The abuser didn't honestly suggest that - they love me.

Quite frequently while the abuser is confronted with their wrongdoing, they resort to denial, or they'll let you know that they love you, and didn't suggest to harm you. It is wishful wondering if you agree with that your abuser victimizes you due to the fact they love you so much that they can't manage themselves. Understand this - it doesn't rely how a whole lot your abuser tells you that they love you. If they do not anything to truly trade their abusive nature, then they may be simply the usage of 'love' as a tactic to control you. They do now not love you. They need to control you and use you to take their frustrations out on.

If they absolutely loved you, they might by no means deal with you this way. And while no person is perfect, a person who's virtually remorseful for hurting you will take motion to end their harmful conduct for appropriate. So, prevent telling yourself that your abuser hurts you due to the fact they love you. They don't. You need to love your self. And if you love yourself you'll take the needed steps to get yourself out of this mess.

If the sufferer complies with their abusers desires the abuser could alternate.

Verbal abusers are routine in telling their sufferers that things might get better if the victim changed their conduct, or stopped doing things the abuser doesn't like. If you are being emotionally abused, and your abuser keeps telling you that they could stop yelling at you if you didn't bother them at the same time as watching tv, or they wouldn't call you 'fat $%&!' in case you lost weight, then they may be mendacity to you. Abusers don't need to exchange their conduct, which is why they maintain putting special conditions for the victim to abide by using. If the sufferer follows one rule, they come up with another. So, even if you did some thing your abuser asked of you, believing in true faith that your gestures could change them, please recognize that an abuser will constantly find some thing else they are able to use to try to manage you. If the abuser wanted to alternate, they wouldn't set ever changing situations so that it will abide by way of because love doesn't come with situations.

Now that we've got mentioned some of the myths related to emotional abuse, and what makes up psychological abuse, you ought to be capable of without difficulty perceive what those sorts of abuse appear to be. And in case you are tormented by emotional abuse, you could begin taking steps to do something about it nowadays.

UNDERSTANDING MANIPULATION, CONTROLLING BEHAVIOR, AND ITS CAUSES

Controlling behavior is commonly exhibited by means of many kinds of abusers. So, it would not be a stretch to mention that your abuser most likely has a controlling character, and attempts to alter each pass you make.

Most don't understand the signs and symptoms that someone is attempting to manipulate and manage them until it's far too late due to the fact the manipulation has a tendency to progress through the years. A manipulator knows that in the event that they try to exert too much manipulate over you inside the early ranges of your courting it is going to be both jarring and alarming and you could cease the relationship.

Moreover, manipulators will frequently check you to peer how some distance they can go with you. They will keenly observe you till they learn precisely the way to make the most you to their very own ends. Manipulators are patient predators who will make the effort to study your vulnerabilities, and could observe the way you react to them and others around you. A manipulator desires your believe, and if you want to turn out to be depending on them.

Controlling people additionally have a propensity to allow their imaginations to combination with fact. They do not react, reply, or behave in a everyday manner because something they see, experience, pay attention, and think is warped on its adventure thru their personal fantasy global. They yearn to dictate every and each flow weaker people around them make. Treating their victims like youngsters. They preference to make every important and trivial decision of the weaker person's existence, and will get disillusioned if the character they're trying to manipulate doesn't do matters their way.

Controlling human beings don't see the arena as it's far or different humans as they're. They need to outline others. They assume human beings to comply to their arbitrary rules, and rules. These human beings interpret reality differently in which certain words and movements have a exclusive meaning to them than what different people could outline things as. And they without difficulty get upset when truth intrudes on their interpretation of the world. When this takes place, they may do whatever it takes to force fact again consistent with their fantasy world. They accomplish this by way of implementing their will on the human beings closets to them, ordinarily on their own family and spouse.

But what reasons them to act like this? Keep reading to discover.

Why Do People Control And Manipulate Others?

Research and scientific research have shown that controlling humans behave in a certain way because of one or more of the subsequent motives.

Difficult adolescence

A fundamental reason behind the manipulative mind-set of your controlling abuser can be the end result of a tough youth. The abuser won't have acquired the love, care, and nourishment youngsters want at a younger age from their mother and father or guardians. Or they skilled their mother and father or guardians behave in a controlling way towards themselves and/or others. Instead of being showered with affection and encouragement, and love they have been controlled by their dad and mom. When they noticed their parents behaving in an abusive way, they wrongly learned that it become the right and handiest manner to act, and as adults, they followed the same dangerous conduct.

Suffered from a considerable loss

Another reason in the back of their dominating behavior will be a considerable loss they suffered within the beyond. Either they suffered from a big blow, or lost something or someone important to them making them experience that they must manipulate you, or else they will emerge as dropping you as nicely. Additionally, they will experience that they have been harm sufficient, and that they won't deliver this right to every body else ever again.

And this is why they start controlling the entirety and every person important in their lifestyles, so no person has the electricity to hurt them once more.

They feel insecure

Quite regularly, controlling and oppressive human beings have insecurities hidden deep interior them. They ought to have low shallowness, negative self-self assurance and several different weaknesses that they want to maintain hidden from others, that's why they start controlling human beings round them. This facilitates them expel the frustrations associated with their shortcomings, and veil their insecurities.

To assist their ego

Some controlling human beings exhibit manipulative behavior for you to improve their ego. This makes them feel powerful and sturdy, which gives them a surge of delight.

Fear of losing and being imperfect

Quite often, dominating people are perfectionists and want everyone and the whole thing round them to be perfect. Since they may be familiar with prevailing and having everything in the precise order, they start controlling human beings around them, with a purpose to best them as nicely. It is in all likelihood your abuser displays a dominating conduct due to this cause in the event that they hold telling you ways incorrect you are, and which you need to try being ideal like them.

Underlying conditions and issues

Suffering from an underlying condition, or an emotional disease is any other motive at the back of controlling conduct. Disorders inclusive of histrionic persona disease, paranoid persona disorder, based persona ailment, borderline personality disorder, delinquent persona disease, narcissistic character disease, avoidant personality ailment, and obsessive compulsive persona disease are a number of the issues that may result in controlling behavior. These conditions and issues make an abuser control you and others round them, that allows you to cope with their situation. Quite often, they aren't even aware of their situation, and don't even know they are affected by a critical mental ailment.

When you intently analyze the reasons outlined above, you'll see that you simply do now not play any position in making your abuser behave the way that they do. Their personal personal problems lead them to behave this manner, and it is not your fault at all. So, you MUST prevent blaming yourself, and recognize that your abuser does not assume or behave like a normal man or woman.

Myths Associated With Controlling Behavior

Here are the not unusual fallacies connected with controlling and manipulative conduct.

Controlling behavior is an indication of passion.

Some humans and societies believe that if a person is controlling you, it's far because they're in reality passionate about you. Nobody has the proper to control all and sundry to such an quantity that they dictate every circulate you're making. Moreover, having intense love and passion for a person don't give everybody the excuse to dominate you.

Controlling behavior isn't a massive deal.

It is likewise believed that controlling behavior isn't a huge deal because the abuser is most effective affecting your actions and they are able to't control your thoughts. However, controlling behavior has huge implications on you and your existence. If a person is controlling you, your perception gadget and mindset stands the chance of come to be permanently altered. Therefore, you have to no longer fall into the entice of believing that the controlling behavior proven via your abuser isn't a regarding difficulty. Instead, you ought to to apprehend how devastating it may be in your lifestyles, and do something positive about it.

Your abuser has your first-class pursuits at coronary heart.

As with verbal abuse, many believe that a controlling individual controls only desires to manage you because they've your satisfactory pursuits at heart. This is false. If they did have your exceptional pastimes at coronary heart, they could deal with you with appreciate, and can help you make decisions on your own rather than supplying you with no preference in the rely.

Only men exhibit controlling behavior.

This notion is incorrect due to the fact there are many girls who manipulate their families, and their spouses. Therefore, both the genders have the potential to show off controlling conduct.

Now that we've got protected a number of the myths associated with controlling conduct, let's study some manipulative tactics controlling human beings use that bring about its recipients turning into sufferers of emotional abuse and psychological violence.

Chapter 2: Insight Into Different Types Of

Manipulative Behaviors

There are exceptional sorts of manipulators, manipulative behaviors, and controlling relationships. It is critical to apprehend the differences, so that you can pin point what types of manipulate and manipulation you experiencing. This know-how will arm you with perception so you can deal with your scenario successfully.

Common behavioral traits and manipulative behaviors exhibited by way of controlling manipulative humans are as follows:

Narcissistic Behavior: Narcissistic conduct is displayed by human beings with narcissistic persona disease. These humans have this sort of high regard for themselves that they want and need anyone to recognize them. The narcissist is so worried with having every person appreciate them and their accomplishments, that they lack all situation and empathy for others. If your controller well-knownshows this behavior, you'll regularly locate them praising their very own competencies. They aren't able to see the best in every body else but themselves, and they'll never recognize your strengths or abilities. They are simplest involved approximately themselves and their accomplishments, and could use the people around them for their very own advantage. Moreover, they may constantly are seeking attention and admiration from you, and others round them. All in their relationships, which includes their intimate and sexual relationships are superficial. Those relationships exist handiest to enhance the narcissist's shallowness.

In addition to the above, they may also show off certain pathological behaviors. For example, if they may be your companion or partner, they may will be predisposed to act in severe methods towards you and showcase sadistic behavior. Parents, spouses, and siblings exhibiting this behavior can grow to be extremely insulting and have a tendency to publicly humiliate you, on the way to make their selves experience superior to you.

Childish Infantile Behavior: If your abuser shows this behavior, they may be probably to throw tantrums, to make you observe their demands. If you try disagreeing with them, they may begin shouting, crying, or throwing horrible fits to disappointed you. In efforts to calm them down, you sooner or later provide in to their needs and needs. People who show infantile infantile conduct need you to sense sorry for them, so that you follow their needs. Resulting of their last goal which is to manipulate and manage you. Like children, these human beings need the world to bend to their fantasies and dreams, and will act out while truth confronts them head on.

Pathological qualities they exhibit consist of throwing tantrums publicly, telling lies approximately you, and they'll even move as a long way as accusing you of harming them physically, in order that human beings view you as the dominant character, and become showing sympathy to your abuser.

Histrionic Behavior: This behavior is similar to narcissistic behavior. Controllers exhibiting this conduct continuously seeks interest and praise from others, are extremely dramatic, emotional or sexually provocative, are strongly opinionated, but may be effortlessly inspired by way of others. They also are incredibly involved with their bodily appearance, and their emotions alternate hastily. If they're in a courting, they generally tend to become attached to the opposite person manner too quickly, and they accept as true with that they've possession over the object in their affection. However, the difference between the histrionic and narcissistic man or woman is that histrionics can be encouraged by using others, while narcissists don't price everybody else sufficient to be motivated through them.

Pathological characteristics histrionic humans display include using intercourse and sexual behavior as a tool to control you, and clinging to you 24/7 because they feel you are their assets.

Additional methods manipulators might also use may be as overt as threatening someone verbally, or as subtle as choreographing external instances in approaches that want the manipulators agenda. For example, many manipulators like to turn two pals against each other. They want to make one buddy consider that the opposite is spreading lies towards them and speaking about them negatively in the back of their returned. This breeds mistrust, and gives the manipulator manipulate over the way the friends interact and understand each different. It additionally makes the pals extra depending on the manipulator because they now look at the manipulator as a agree with worth ally and their friend as a capability enemy. When in truth the manipulator is the enemy who is the usage of these people to meet their very own wishes.

Another tactic a manipulative man or woman might also use is by promising to position an stop to a conduct that they realize you don't like. For example they may say "I promise I might be better and prevent XYX. All I want for you do is that this one desire for me. Please, I simply need your assist this one closing time." You need to recognize that there will usually be a next time. Alternatively, they'll inform you "If you maintain doing X / or don't do X, then I am going to do Y. And I don't need to do this to you. Don't make me do that to you. I love you."

Other techniques a manipulator may also use may additionally to manipulate you may be competitive like shouting, lying, bullying, pretending to be indignant with you, name-calling, or intimidation. On the opposite hand, greater passive techniques a manipulator may additionally use to control you are the silent treatment, sulking, pouting, and ignoring you. These are all attempts by using the manipulator to make you bend to their will, and exert electricity and control over your thoughts and moves.

With the above in mind, some thing very vital to reiterate is that these behavioral characteristics stem shape underlying character problems. Some people mistakenly accept as true with that they are able to trade their abuser. However, frequently times the abuser doesn't even realize what they are doing or why. These humans need professional help, and you could't alternate them.

Chapter 3: Different Kinds Of Controlling Relationships And The Right Way To Deal With Them

Controlling conduct is regularly believed to be constrained to the connection shared with the aid of two spouses or intimate companions. However, this couldn't be in addition from the reality. Although, many human beings wind up coping with controlling humans and suffering from emotional abuse while they are dating, or when they get married, let us now not forget about about those who are controlled via their mother and father, siblings, loved ones, coworkers, pals and bosses. Let us take a closer look into those relationships. Identifying unique tactics an abuser may use to govern you, and discussing simple techniques that can be used to successfully put an cease to controlling conduct.

Problems Experienced In A Controlling Relationship

If you are in a controlling courting, be it together with your parent, sibling, friend(s) or intimate associate, and are being ruled by them, then you may easily relate to descriptions referred to in earlier chapters. Your complete existence may be depending on your abuser due to the fact they do no longer assist you to do some thing to your personal. It is probable that they're completely in rate of dealing with the price range of the residence, and pressure you to be completely reliant on them for money. In addition, they are quite probably to decide the subjects you ought to examine, the career direction you should pick, whether or not or now not you need to paintings, whom you must have interaction with, and whom you need to marry (if that character is your determine or elder dominant sibling). Some even go as far as what you need to wear, say, and consume (typically, while the controlling man or woman is your spouse or dictating parent).

Living in this case makes you feel worthless because you don't have the proper to do anything the manner you desire, and are possibly to face grim consequences within the shape of verbal abuse, manipulation, psychological trauma, or maybe even physical abuse in case you don't abide by way of their policies. When you experience like you haven't any manage over your life, you become bored in it, and your existence turns into some thing to bear and not experience. Additionally, whilst you aren't allowed to decide things for yourself, your self-confidence additionally begins to dwindle. The moment your self belief declines, you stop believing in your self, and in any life desires you formerly set for yourself. You stop pursuing dreams and objectives due to the fact your simplest ultimate objective is to satisfy the needs of the controlling man or woman to your life. In time, your happiness degree decrease, and you start teetering at the verge of persistent stress and melancholy.

The exact information is that lifestyles doesn't should be this way. If you're bored with living this way, if you want to move on, live happily and freely, and put a permanent stop to this situation, it's miles critical which you apprehend that you are not guilty for the controlling conduct inflicted on you. Moreover, there are moves you may take today to quit the manipulate that a manipulator has over you.

Family

Numerous cases had been said in which the controlling behavior in an abusive dating became perpetrated via the mother and father, guardians, or siblings of the victim.

Remember that a manipulator likes to have strength over others, and that they assert this strength via the use of controlling, dominating, and subjugating behavior. Manipulators gain by this fostering immoderate stages of guilt, fear, embarrassment, and disgrace of their sufferers. They manage your emotions and perceptions through constant humiliation and denial. When symptoms of your abuse start becoming obvious to others your manipulator will lie, and try and convince others which you are the only with intellectual health issues. Resulting in further isolation of their victims.

Manipulators additionally prey on the ones which might be the most vulnerable like aged, unwell, or infirm family. And they will additionally prey on the ones that are the most emotionally needy like kids. In reality, children are usually to suffer from approaches like being blamed for life conditions which can be out of their manipulate, being omitted, no longer allowed to have pals, name calling, being continuously criticized and made fun of, or being pressured to carry out degrading acts.

Manipulators really are sadistic emotional assassins, who obtain gratification from frightening own family individuals to fight, and have interaction in destructive behavior. When you're distracted through steady inter familial conflicts interest is drawn faraway from the real supply of the trouble – the manipulator.

If your dad and mom or siblings are seeking to dominate you, right here's how you may discover their controlling behavior:

• They insist on determining matters for you, consisting of what type of education, lifestyles path, and profession you need to pursue.

• They manage your budget, and could not will let you open your personal bank account while you are of prison adult age.

• They will now not let you pressure yourself, and demand on losing you off anywhere you need to go, and are constantly checking your phone.

• They constantly humiliate you, and belittle your features and strengths, regularly times inside the presence of others.

• They don't provide you with the right to talk in the front of them, or explicit your own perspectives.

How You Can Fight Back:

• Don't play their sport.

• Don't have interaction them.

• Define verbalize and put in force boundaries.

• Let the individual recognise that there are new rules for attractive and interacting with you. One way to do this is with the aid of enforcing a time body whereby you both take a destroy from the relationship. It may be 30 days it may be 60 days. It's up to you. Communicate this to them. If they could't recognize the time table then restart the clock until they respect it.

• Act confident. They want to recognize you are extreme.

• Don't feel responsible - that is an emotion that they use to govern you with.

• If the man or woman doesn't change their behavior you could have to re-compare the connection, or even end it.

• Forgive the character. So you can pass on In existence, and nonetheless be open to reconnecting in the event that they change.

Partner/Spouse

Many ladies and men enjoy emotional abuse in intimate relationships with a associate or spouse each 12 months. If you are in a dating with a controlling individual, here's how you can spot it early on.

• They continually ask you for wonderful feedback on their look and characteristics.

• They are always sharing their experiences and memories in their accomplishments with you, however by no means let you speak.

• They use your phrases in opposition to you in approaches that questions your truthfulness and recollection.

• They grow to be enormously infuriated while you don't concentrate to them, whilst you are late assembly them, or while matters they requested you to do take longer than predicted.

• They use your vulnerabilities, weaknesses, and insecurities towards you to hurt and manipulate you.

• They yell and criticize you, can call you disrespectful and disparaging names.

• They are continuously supplying you with orders, however aren't willing to take any from you.

• If they locate any chance to humiliate you, and quickly capitalize it.

If your boyfriend/lady friend displays those behaviors, you need to research your courting with them and quit it right away, so you can save you them from completely controlling you.

How You Can Fight Back:

• Start with yourself - Understand your rights. Decide what you need out of the relationship. Do you want to live or leave?

• Be inclined to leave if necessary.

• Have a guide system in area.

• Be prepared for terrible and superb effects.

• Ask for assist.

• Ask your abuser questions like:

o "Does this request sound affordable to you?"

o "Does this request sound honest to me?

o "Are you asking me or telling me?"

o "So, what do I get out of doing this?"

o "Do you significantly anticipate me to do...?

Colleagues/Boss

Quite often, colleagues and executives try to control you as well. Here are the early signs and symptoms to be privy to so you can spot those emotional assassins.

• Your boss is always rude to you, and dictatorial.

• Your boss by no means appreciates the paintings you do, and humiliates you in front of others.

• Your boss shouts at you, and wrongly accuses you of negative overall performance.

• Your colleagues twist and spin your words in ways that questions your truthfulness and recollection in an try to outshine you in the front of your superiors.

• Your colleagues are usually making jokes at your fee, and deal with you want an interloper.

• Your colleagues find out your weaknesses, and attempt to control you by way of the usage of them as bribes to make the most you.

How You Can Fight Back:

• Don't have interaction your abuser.

• Tell you abuser that you arc busy, and don't have time to talk.

• Stand up for yourself (nation what you'll and will not take delivery of or tolerate from them).

• Learn to say no.

• Remain calm, file, record to HR.

• Communicate via e mail for documentation if vital.

Friends

Controlling relationships also can exists among buddies. Manipulators are brilliant at getting you to divulge heart's contents to them, and reveal your maximum intimate thoughts and insecurities. They recognize that it feels precise to speak to someone, and to have a person listen to you with undivided attention. But pay attention. Their real reason is to locate ways to control you. They will use your weak spot and insecurities to make you feel beholden to them and responsible in case you try to face up to giving into their needs. Leaving you careworn and hurt.

If any of your pals dominate you, is impolite to you, abuses you, and continuously makes use of you to gain their personal ends, then they aren't genuine honest pals. They are emotionally abusing you. Early signs and symptoms of this controlling behavior in a friendship include:

• Your buddies make a laugh of you constantly, and speak to you humiliating names.

• They use your weakness to control you.

• They solicit huge favors from you, and in case you don't pay heed to their orders, they threaten to reveal your weaknesses on your parents or the world.

How You Can Fight Back:

• Set your barriers.

• Learn to say no.

• Become someone who can't be manipulated - greater on this In the subsequent bankruptcy.

Dealing With The Tactics Your Abuser Uses

This phase will talk a number of the maximum common approaches emotional assassins and manipulative humans use to get their manner,

41

and effective ways to cope with them. Before confronting or handling your abuser you have to prepare your self mentally so that you don't get frazzled by using their controlling presence. You must come to be like steel. Don't sense sorry for them, or get sucked in via their methods and tries to manipulate you. Here is what to do once they motel to:

• Throwing Tantrums: If your mental abuser has a addiction of throwing suits, you then must deal with them very lightly. Stay calm while they may be throwing a tantrum, and don't react, due to the fact you don't need them to grow to be physically violent. After they may be completed with their tantrum and have calmed down, speak to them and inform them in a polite but company voice that their behavior is unacceptable and also you aren't putting up with it any extra.

Only if display real regret, ought to you don't forget and speak methods to help them. If they show no regret and deny their abuse, set boundaries for them, and give an explanation for the effects for no longer obeying the ones obstacles. Ensure that you put into effect the effects to make the abuser recognize that you are serious.

• Lying: If your abuser tells lies about you, you collect evidence to aid your argument, and tell them that you realize they're mendacity and have proof, and should remember revising their model of factors. However, make certain to reply to their lies in a peaceful style, and never emerge as irritated with them. Use your frame language, and tone of voice to talk which you don't believe them, and that their make consider memories do no longer affect you.

Clique Forming: Colleagues and insincere friends normally motel to this behavior. If a number of your coworkers or friends decide they don't like you and begin to shape cliques - ignore them. Be courteous to them, so there's no tension among you, but ignore their infantile behavior. Don't let them recognise that their conduct affects you.

Focus on your paintings and accomplishing your dreams. Show them which you don't want to be round with folks who behave like them anyway. If essential discover a new activity, and cling out with other pals. If you don't have any nice friendships it is time to cultivate new ones.

Threatening and Blaming: If your abuser threatens and blames you, you need to confront them and inform them that you are aware of what they're attempting to do, that it'll now not work, and you'll not take it anymore. Be corporation and polite with them, but make certain to keep direct eye contact with them. Do no longer show weakness. If they deny it, allow them to know which you are sure of what you're pronouncing, and will no longer permit them to preserve with their abuse.

Next, set limitations for them, and tell them what they ought to and ought to no longer do with you, how they can act and the way they cannot act with you, and what you will and will no longer be given from them. Also, explain to them the effects they'll face if they preserve treating you in a way that you may now not be given, consisting of a separation or divorce (inside the case of companion/partner), leaving them (within the case of parents/ siblings), reporting their conduct to HR (within the case of an abusive boss or colleagues), and reporting them to the police (within the case of all the abusive relationships mentioned above). If they retain with the abuse, you need to put into effect the consequence(s) you warned them of so one can see that you are serious.

By using those methods you will be on the direction to ending the manipulative conduct by the emotional murderer on your lifestyles. And you will be in the direction of accomplishing the healthy lifestyles which you deserve.

HOW TO NEVER FALL VICTIM TO MANIPULATIVE PEOPLE AND EMOTIONAL ASSASSINS EVER AGAIN

Falling victim to manipulative controlling human beings and emotional abuse are in no way your fault. And no one should ever deal with you that way. However, due to the fact there are human beings that are searching for to take benefit of others and prey on perceived weaknesses you need to take steps to ensure you by no means fall victim to these sorts of predators once more. How?

First allow's move over a few common developments that manipulators search for, and that make you liable to their approaches.

Traits That Make You Vulnerable To Manipulation

• Needing to be popular and authorized of with the aid of others.

• Needing to take care of others so as to experience beneficial.

• Shying away from warfare and confrontation, and being frightened of expressing terrible emotions.

• Unable to say no to others even when a state of affairs is horrific for you.

• Not being capable of set clear boundaries that outline who you're and what you stand for.

• Being uncertain of your values, and no longer trusting your judgement.

Now, please apprehend that the above trends do now not make you a awful person, or deserving of abuse. I had to overcome some of them myself. But by being privy to what manipulative human beings search for on the way to take gain of different human beings will shield you even as you are still in the method of self-discovery.

Protect Yourself From Manipulation

When confronted with manipulative people on your lifestyles here are some pointers which can aide in organising the dynamics of your relationships.

Instead of focusing on converting the manipulator awareness on your self.

You handiest have manage over the way you reply to the person manipulating you. You can't out control them. And telling them how you experience received't work. Sadly, they may be most effective concerned with their feelings, and sharing yours will handiest give them extra ammunition to use against you in the destiny. By focusing on the dynamics of the relationship you preserve and maintain your strength. And manipulators admire power.

Determine how vital the relationship is to you.

If you watched a person of seeking to control you determine if the relationship is worth it to hold. If now not, permit it pass if possible. You don't need that in your life. If it's far a family member that you may't without problems disconnect with discern out what you need out of the relationship, and establish floor policies.

Use assertive strategies to regain control over yourself and the scenario.

You can do that with the aid of finding exclusive methods to respond humans's needs of you. For instance use time in your benefit. Instead of robotically pronouncing yes to requests of you, begin announcing some thing like "I'll consider it, and get returned to you." Congratulations, you have got taken back manage! But don't be fooled your manipulator will try to get it lower back. So, if asked why you need time don't deliver reasons just preserve to mention "I want greater time to suppose, and I gets returned to you." Keep repeating that word, and don't supply in even though they hold asking you. And if making a decision you cannot comply examine to say "No."

Confront all of the motives why you said yes in the past.

Is it worry, guilt, tension? You will need to look at your self for these reasons.

Use direct eye touch whilst you speak.

It makes you look, and sense on top of things.

When communicating with someone you observed of being controlling, and manipulative talk to them in a relaxed company voice.

Tell them that you understand that they may be attempting to manipulate you, however that it isn't always going to paintings on you. If they need to maintain handling you they will have to tell you what they want in a respectful way, and can help you determine what you want to do transferring forward.

These are not clean steps to take, so if vital are seeking out the help of a expert for help.

Chapter 4: So, What Is Selfishness Anyway?

Being the opposite of altruism and selflessness, selfishness essentially refers to having an immoderate or unique issue for one's personal desires, satisfaction, and health, regardless of what this could suggest for those around us. Some have pointed out that selfishness may mean a lack of empathy, and in a few instances, can be a result of manipulation for self-gain.

When we talk over with selfishness, it's crucial to observe that there are healthy levels of selfishness. In order to live on, all of us want to keep a certain degree of self-care and self-issue. In fact, addressing one's own wishes is crucial to any sort of success, and is the guiding principle of fundamental survival. Selfishness only takes a flip for the worst whilst we start to disregard the welfare of others that allows you to ensure our personal happiness. Unhealthy selfishness is what we must are looking for to avoid, as it is the cause of many more conflicts; from

51

interpersonal conflicts to conflicts between countries and the world at huge.

Unhealthy selfishness isn't to be taken in isolation from other self-centered behaviors either. Unhealthy selfishness can permeate and rework into behaviors like greediness, narcissism, egocentrism, manipulation and manipulate problems.

WHAT ARE THE EFFECTS OF SELFISHNESS?

In an individualistic world, selfishness won't sound so bad to a few. While being egocentric doesn't right away imply that you are a terrible man or woman, dangerous selfishness does have some negative effects that wreck relationships and act as detriments to someone's universal well-being.

Here are a few results of dangerous levels of selfishness:

-Destruction of Relationships:

Relationships of their most simple sense contain a partnership among people. In order for a dating to thrive and survive, companions should display at the same time fantastic behavior like the willingness to compromise, concern for the alternative's needs. Selfishness, on the other hand, is a one-manner street. It entails worrying for the self and the self by myself, some thing this may encompass. Concern most effective for one's own desires approach setting others second or setting others last, regardless of context.

Those in relationships with egocentric human beings often describe emotions of helplessness, overlook, and inferiority. Many times the selfish birthday party ignores the emotions of his or her companion, or minimizes their proceedings and their needs a good way to stable his or her very own role inside the courting dynamic. When requested, the selfish companion will most probable deny or even have hassle recognizing a hassle in the dating in any respect, no matter how tons their accomplice is absolutely already suffering.

Abusive relationships (emotional or physical) regularly have this type of dynamic. Because the giving associate is so often denied of being heard, they begin to naturally take an inferior position or attitude. Problems accentuate while the abused accomplice starts offevolved to take at the mentality of the abusive man or woman; as a result denying as well that any issues may additionally exist inside the dating. This ends in the perpetuation of abuse, rooted within the selfishness of the other in his or her need to stay "in electricity".

-Objectification of Others:

Many selfish human beings regularly turn out to be very entrenched in their very own worlds that they start to view relationships as something comparable to transactions. People emerge as turning into objectified, or valued best in terms of what they could provide/give in go back. Selfish humans might also have a tendency to objectify human beings they come across; no longer recognizing them as complete individuals however most effective judging them with the aid of whether they may be "of use" or no longer, or what benefits they could provide.

This may be a trouble now not most effective in intimate relationships or friendships, but additionally at work. For instance, having a boss who has this attitude may additionally demand irrational ranges of perfection from his personnel, and might straight away judge a subordinate badly when they make errors. This can also lead to abusive situations, and is usually a concept mentioned when speaking about sexual harassment.

-Dishonesty & Manipulative Behavior:

Remember that dangerous stages of selfishness contain searching out for one's personal well being, regardless of whether this means stepping on different human beings along the way. Common examples of cheating and manipulative behavior contain a power dynamic.

For instance, take the situation of Boss A and Employee B. Boss A asks Employee B to perform a little studies on corporate mastering, and to make a presentation approximately the way to better improve the business enterprise's modern studying and development packages. Employee B does his task nicely, and makes an powerful and meaningful presentation. If Boss A is egocentric and would like to develop his personal recognition in the organisation, he will take the presentation for his very own and fail to give credit score/popularity to Employee B.

In this case, it's far possibly that given Boss A's role and tenure over his subordinate, Employee B will simply preserve quiet and no longer talk approximately his worries with every body. However, if Boss A has wholesome tiers of selfishness, he'll recognize the difficult paintings of Employee B, and will have the maturity to apprehend that the performance of his subordinate is likewise an amazing reflection on the steering that he gave as a frontrunner.

This also can occur in college amongst peers working together. For example, Student A might also withhold statistics from Student B (both operating on the equal presentation) on a positive subject matter so that you can appear extra informed while the time comes for a public presentation or check. While many people often permit things like those slide given that there was technically no "lie", it's miles already a form of manipulation and deception.

-Inability to Collaborate:

Given how selfishness manifests itself in exceptional conditions, it is often the case that selfish people locate it hard to collaborate. Though they'll locate it easy to call for things of other human beings, they discover it hard to honestly paintings well with others (which calls for compromise, trust, and inequality). They will frequently recognition best on their personal gain, and may make them very touchy in terms of allowing others to proportion the "limelight" when it comes to the completed products. They will have trouble relinquishing control, and could frequently want things to move exactly the manner they need. This makes it very difficult to construct partnerships among colleagues, school associates, or pals.

-Increased Aggressiveness or Disagreeableness

Selfish humans may be more susceptible to act out or to be extra competitive towards others, especially in situations where different humans may be viewed as a danger to at least one's present day stature.

-Infidelity in Relationships:

Selfishness also can rear its ugly head within the form of infidelity. It's critical to understand that being in a relationship doesn't suggest that every one different temptations disappear while you make a commitment. However, selfishness makes these commitments vulnerable within the face of temptations which are gift along the manner. Infidelity might also thoroughly be a end result of selfishness, inside the feel that the dishonest birthday party disregards his or her companion and will are trying to find to meet the choice for activity outside the connection they're already in. It isn't that the temptation was too strong; it's due to the fact the individual was too egocentric to mention no to the temptation, and was too egocentric to see beyond himself or herself. Taken inside the context of selfishness, infidelity is a blatant push aside for the feelings of others for one's personal benefit.

-Helplessness

One interesting conduct that could end result from selfishness is becoming helpless, or feigning helplessness, in one-of-a-kind conditions. For a self-worried person, being helpless may imply that someone near them will attend to their needs, or maybe do things for them. Eventually, egocentric people may also examine that performing helpless or being helpless equates to their cherished ones dropping everything and going for walks to their aid. Many instances, this will become a pattern; selfish human beings will tend to disregard the weight that this places on their loved ones and maintain capitalizing on this association. In turn, they'll learn how to come to be helpless and surely look forward to others to remedy their problems for them, seeing that helplessness really receives them what they need.

-Ideas of Grandeur and Entitlement

While thinking big isn't constantly a terrible element, egocentric humans may tend to overestimate or exaggerate on what they're capable of doing. They become very competitive, and will tend to be very wary of the notion of others. They can also often need to feel that they're the first-class, and they want other humans to align their perceptions with that as well.

Selfish humans may additionally fall prey to the attitude that they're entitled to their fulfillment. Rather than view other people as worthy competitors, they will really view them as much less deserving. This attitude can result in laziness, and the lack of ability to cope with failure.

-Isolation:

Selfishness doesn't simplest ruin the self. It also alienates other people. Selfish humans can be tolerated through the ones around them, however making proper connections and relationships may be hard. People really don't want that kind of terrible and draining power around them, and selfish human beings are often construed as poisonous or toxic to one's well being.

It is regularly the case that egocentric people have fleeting or brief relationships. As turned into mentioned in advance, selfishness can put a splendid burden on others. Selfish humans can drain different people of resources, and can reason an emotional exhaustion in those they get near. Therefore, relationships regularly generally tend to stop badly and speedy.

These are simply a number of the outcomes of egocentric behavior on the individual psyche, and the way selfishness can affect someone's potential to relate with different human beings on a genuine degree.

Another interesting dating to be aware is the relationship among selfishness and the capability to be satisfied, so as to be mentioned in the next phase.

SELFISHNESS AND HAPPINESS

All of us try to pursue happiness, and every body have felt genuine happiness at least at one factor in our lives. While we continuously war to fulfill our very own wants and needs in our lifelong look for proper contentment, we generally tend to forget that the key to happiness doesn't entirely lie within ourselves.

Behavioral research have shown that a key aspect for ushering happiness into our lives is gratitude. This method spotting the jobs our loved ones play in our lives, and understanding that our private successes also are stimulated via the assist and guide of those around us. Another associated key issue for happiness is selflessness, in place of selfishness. Happiness can be found now not in how a lot we get, however through how a lot we give to those around us. In many ways, proper happiness comes while we see the genuine and actual happiness of the people we've got touched, or the human beings whom have touched us. While a number of us might imagine that giving of ourselves lessens what we've got, the truth is the opposite. When we supply selflessly, we benefit plenty greater than the attention can see; we gain happiness, contentment, and cause in knowing that we've made a wonderful effect on those round us.

It is clear with the aid of now that happiness doesn't always suggest getting what we need. In reality, any other key element to happiness is getting to know to just accept what's given to us, and mastering to make the maximum of our present state of affairs. However, selfishness again acts contrary to this. Selfishness frequently leads us to constantly chasing after our very own goals, and our personal needs, no matter the opposition round us or irrespective of whom we hurt. Therefore, selfish people have a tendency to have less resilience in the face of disappointments or failure. Every situation will become a battle, and failure is now not viewed as a getting to know revel in.

Accepting the antique adage that we will't have the whole lot is in reality a key thing to happiness, and selfishness prevents us from for the reason that.

Coupled with the terrible results of egocentric behavior mentioned inside the preceding element, it's far clean to peer that selfishness isn't only a single, unfavourable behavior; it becomes a vicious cycle that traps a person into constantly chasing after a deeper experience of pleasure that isn't manageable by way of focusing simplest at the self. Selfishness most effective serves to perpetuate self benefit, so it's essential that we learn how to be more open and aware about the want and desires of our cherished ones in place of just our very own.

SELFISHNESS AND LEADERSHIP IN THE WORKPLACE

In relationships, we tend to recognize proper off the bat that selfishness isn't an excellent component. We hear it all the time; egocentric humans don't make right companions, or a selfish courting will in no way training session. In the administrative center but, it's specific. More regularly than no longer, selfishness is considered as a necessity for achievement. Becoming a chairman comes with growing above the ranks, and has a tendency to be associated with setting your self first before every body else. But upon nearer inspection, given what we already recognize, we ought to start to query whether or not selfishness is a hassle rather than an advantage while aiming to emerge as a frontrunner within the workplace.

Before anything else, it's vital to reiterate that selfishness isn't constantly terrible. There are times whilst it is essential to guard and attend to our very own wishes and pastimes, in particular whilst those also assist us make contributions to the corporations or teams that we're part of. We all have to attend to a ourselves to a positive extent so that it will cope with others, and so as to lead others as excellent we are able to. However, as we already realize, selfishness can turn out to be a dangerous element when it comes in excess.

Why are selfish leaders resented by their human beings? Simply due to the fact egocentric human beings behave in ways that undermine morale and any advantageous corporate lifestyle the business enterprise desires to deliver.

Most people have in all likelihood had reviews working with a selfish superior or chief who:

-Steals ideas to create a fantastic affect on higher control; maximum of whom are often now not concerned in the each day operation of a specific team.

-Takes sole credit score for tasks that required the concerted attempt of the group. Although a frontrunner's task is to supervise and to guide every group member, this by no means method that she or he by myself ought to be the face of the entire initiative.

-Shifts the blame for some thing she or he must have performed. Most frequently, higher management delegates tasks to crew leaders, and the crew leaders need to be able to delegate duties to his/her crew participants so one can accomplish the larger obligations on time. They ought to be capable of put into effect a machine within their groups so as to deliver on the bigger picture.

If selfish leaders are unable to provide the right guidance, they will not make it seem so that you could upper control. Often, they'll shift the blame and make the team failure seem like a result of terrible performance of their subordinates, as opposed to a end result of terrible leadership. They might also even cross up to now as to identify a selected character as the "weak hyperlink" inside the team, when in reality, this man or woman surely lacked the right course and steerage.

-Dominates meetings with the aid of final closed to the thoughts of others and resisting upward comments (meaning comments from subordinates to their superiors). Team directions may also generally tend to reflect only their desires with out spotting the wishes of each crew member (e.G. Unrealistic dreams, expectations, and so forth.).

-Always thinks she or he is proper; no matter the outcome. The hassle with that is that different reviews grow to be beside the point, and crew members become not able to do any damage manipulate in case they start down the wrong route. Although leaders may be extra tenured or extra experienced, this doesn't imply that they are always proper. This is wherein the crew is available in; they are able to offer perspective and file to their chief that things may not be going as predicted. However, this can best manifest if the leader himself/herself Is open to suggestions and doesn't take offense to things no longer going as they at the start deliberate.

-Acts as a stressor or pressure for demotivation. 90% of the time, groups lead with the aid of egocentric leaders feature in a culture of dangerous opposition and negativity in place of collaboration. Subordinates turn out to be immersed in a subculture of pressure, and that they frequently feel that they're surprisingly by myself in all their endeavors because of the lack of right leadership.

If you are familiar with any of these points, then you definately recognize that a egocentric chief causes numerous misery in the place of business, past just the obvious factor. Employees who want to follow selfish leaders frequently emerge as demotivated and disengaged, main to reduced productivity and efficiency in phrases of overall performance.

CAN YOU DO ANYTHING ABOUT A SELFISH LEADER?

We know that we are able to't control the ones round us, and that we will best manage our personal conduct and our own actions. So, in preference to becoming pointlessly frustrated approximately operating for a selfish boss, it is evident that we want to learn how to manage egocentric humans inside the workplace.

Here are a few recommendations which you want to manage a egocentric chief:

-Think of the Bigger Picture

Working for a egocentric chief doesn't suggest that every one your projects are worthless. It may additionally thoroughly be that you are operating on a undertaking in an effort to benefit your employer as a whole, except that your have a awful leader for the time. Therefore, it's essential that you don't get stuck up inside the minor politics and stresses of your day-to-day dealings with your boss. Always focus on the truth which you're doing something precise for the enterprise, and that selfishness is just a minor hiccup (now not a deal-breaker).

-Highlight their Success

If you need to push your thoughts and nevertheless cause them to occur despite your boss, it's crucial which you play to their weaknesses. For example, if you think a positive product development should be carried out, don't just endorse it out proper and anticipate your boss to get on board. Instead, discuss your idea and in particular highlight how they'll advantage from enforcing your concept. For example, you could promote your concept by using phrasing it like, "I think we should do this as it will surely gain our product line and increase income. You recognize, you ought to be at the forefront of this leap forward, the advertising and marketing heads will love you for it!"

-Frame Feedback Positively

If you observed that the set course may additionally lead your team to failure (based totally on valid statistics, of course), it's crucial which you communicate up even though your leader may not be open on your opinion. Therefore, while giving feedback in your superior, it's critical which you body it positively or in a manner that doesn't come off as a direct assault on your boss.

For instance, you can say, "I liked the advertising plan which you provided for the duration of our divisional assembly. But I'm concerned that people like such and such, may not relate to it on a level that others may. How do you suspect we could make it extra comprehensible for him/her next time? How ought to we tweak it so the ones on the line really get your imaginative and prescient?" This manner, you're capable of sneak in a supplement and fantastic reinforcement even as giving optimistic feedback.

-Stay Cool

Selfish leaders may also be at risk of flare-u.S.Of terrible temper. You, or someone you already know, may have already skilled being scolded or chastised in the front of the complete workplace or in front of other leaders. During instances like these, it's vital which you learn to detach and preserve calm. Remember that these outbursts are extra a reflection of the adulthood level of your superior and now not a reflection on you. Of course, but, it's crucial that you also acknowledge your shortcomings;

however, you shouldn't measure your really worth honestly through how your superior is treating you.

-Avoid Gossiping

When you're being lead through a horrific boss, it's natural so as to try to find support amongst your colleagues with the aid of talking badly approximately your superior and gossiping approximately their every pass. While this could experience like the proper component to do on the time, realize that it isn't. Gossiping gets you nowhere, and may in fact placed your very own credibility at danger. Know that those who often interact in gossip are viewed as untrustworthy and disgruntled, regardless of how valid their proceedings are.

Though it's far perfect to speak about it now and again, be careful no longer to get over excited. Gossiping additionally often reaches higher management degrees, and might have an effect on your viability for merchandising or progress inside the company if you are perceived as a non-crew player.

-Documentation

Picking up from the preceding point, it's essential that you record your court cases and supplement it with valid statistics. When you've got a complaint towards your boss, report it and cite particular activities that illustrate your difficulty. Gossiping doesn't result in improvement; it really perpetuates a culture of mistrust and negativity.

Therefore, recognition on enhancing the scenario with the aid of giving optimistic and well-documented comments (in place of specializing in destroying the popularity of your boss). Furthermore, having documentation of things which have took place within the place of business offers top control or human resources the possibility to create actionable and powerful interventions.

-Speak Up

Managing your boss and preserving them happy has its limits. It's additionally crucial that you apprehend while you simply need to talk up for your self, especially whilst things which might be going on go against your ideals and your values. Remember that retaining silent is a way of condoning the wrong happening round you, so be careful in terms of what you permit appear.

It's additionally critical to be aware that talking up isn't equal to you dropping your temper, or having an outburst. You can constantly make it a constructive session through speaking rationally, and speaking from an area of surely trying to peer change for the betterment of the group.

If you experience that your boss is absolutely closed off to the idea of sitting down with you and having a conversation, try to technique the human sources department of your enterprise or your intermediate advanced (the advanced of your boss).

-Know When to Walk Away

When you experience that selfishness has turn out to be systemic and doesn't most effective prevent along with your boss, you need to don't forget on foot away. Sometimes, there without a doubt are some systems or mindsets which you can not change. If you feel which you are now not growing inside your enterprise because of those sorts of terrible personalities round you, and if you experience that you are not able to do things that gain your profession ultimately, then begin looking for different alternatives. Remember that that is the instant in which you have to start considering your personal pastimes and your own destiny, and making selections to shield that. If you select to leave and pursue different opportunities, make sure to offer comments in the course of your exit interview to offer them perception on what they have to enhance on.

These are simply some of the things that you can do when handling selfish bosses or coworkers. Remember that you may manage your own conduct and how you react to the personalities round you, so take the opportunity to be proactive in building a very good and wholesome career and work surroundings.

Chapter 5: Selfishness In Relationships

Now that we've talked at duration about the results of selfishness and the selfishness in the place of job, it's critical that we communicate approximately selfishness in relationships. Many instances we may not be capable of see the signs and symptoms that we're in a selfish relationship until it's too past due, so being able to understand sure behaviors can save us from needless hurt and pain.

Here are a few pink flags which could shop us from adverse relationships:

-Me, Myself, and I

If you locate that most of your conversations revolve round only your associate, consisting of his/her desires, needs, goals, goals, and many others., then there is a awesome threat which you are in a dating with a selfish character. Though it's regular to percentage non-public statistics with your companion, it needs to be balanced with genuine and energetic listening as properly.

-"How is that interesting?"

It is a for the reason that you'll not like the whole thing your partner likes, and that your associate will not like the whole lot you want. However, if she or he makes no effort in any respect to recognize what attracts you to a positive passion/hobby, or if he/she doesn't even ask approximately it in any respect, you must be concerned. In a partnership, every birthday party have to support the endeavors of the opposite, although it isn't a mutual hobby. Selfish people are often incapable of getting on board with some thing that they could't relate with, so in case you sense that is the case, begin to rethink whether you're courting is heading down a one-way street.

-Doing before Thinking

Another sign is while your partner does different things with out thinking about how it influences you. Again, a relationship is lots approximately compromise and finding common ground. If you find that you're constantly reducing your requirements or pushing aside what you want just to adjust to what your partner wishes, then it's far probable that your associate's behavior is driven simplest by way of his/her personal want and desires.

-Listen to Me!

A definite crimson flag is while your accomplice constantly wishes you to concentrate and provide emotional help, regardless of whether or not you aren't in a nation to achieve this. Many human beings in selfish relationships locate themselves exhausted, virtually due to the fact all their electricity is spent supporting and paying attention to a needy partner, even if they themselves are dealing with a number of problem and strife. Then, when they do talk up and request the same, they're called "selfish" for doing so.

-Relationship Scoreboard

Genuine relationships require giving without counting the value. However, egocentric companions are distinct. They can be beneficiant to you and act that way closer to you, but make no mistake about whether they may be preserving score. Selfish partners regularly supply and assume something in go back, and can hold you responsible for "repaying" them in a single way or another.

-Emotional Blackmail

One painful element of being in a egocentric courting is the tendency for the egocentric associate to motel to emotional blackmail when she or he doesn't get what they need. If your accomplice is selfish, they may take it individually in case you aren't able to provide them the love or attention that they need. If you sense that emotional blackmail is a device that your companion uses if your companion whilst she or he doesn't get what they want, this need to serve as a crimson flag.

-Saying No is Easy

If you're in a selfish relationship, you'll discover that there is lots of hesitation when the situation requires your partner to give or proportion. While we aren't saying that your companion has to mention "yes" to everything which you need or need, it's essential that your partner say accept as true with you or what you want to do for the reason that it is some thing this is wholesome for you and could help you grow in a effective way. Selfish human beings have trouble pronouncing sure when there's nothing in it for them, so if you discover that your companion always says no to things that she or he finds boring, you need to think twice approximately the kingdom of your courting.

-Promises Are Meant to Be Broken

Selfish human beings can also regularly be flaky approximately their commitments, mainly if it's something that doesn't immediately gain them in an obvious manner. If you're in a egocentric relationship, your accomplice might also seem to be unable to take into account commitments he/she made to you, and may continually appear to "overlook" his or her obligations in the context of the relationship.

-Forced Apologies

When we are in relationships, we now and again hurt our partners without meaning to. Or, whilst carried away by means of our feelings, we tend to say things or do matters we subsequently regret. For an unselfish character, the capability to make an apology for doing such things will come obviously. For a selfish person, however, apologies will frequently should be pressured out of them if they experience that the motive isn't comprehensible or legitimate. If you locate that you frequently need to guilt your associate in apologizing to you, then this could be a signal that your accomplice is more selfish than you'd at the beginning concept.

These are simply a number of the symptoms that your associate might also have bad tiers of selfishness, mainly in relation to your relationship. Although it's always an option to stroll away, there are other approaches that you may cope with having a egocentric associate, and selfish human beings in general. These will be mentioned inside the following segment.

DEALING WITH SELFISH PEOPLE

The preceding sections have tackled the difficulties of getting egocentric people around us, and the way those demanding situations can honestly get us down. We understand that at the same time as it's ideal to sincerely disconnect from the poisonous human beings in our lives, this isn't usually possible. Therefore, it's higher to recognize a way to control our relationships and interactions with them.

Here are a few very useful recommendations in managing the pressure of relating with egocentric human beings:

-Address Your Insecurities

Often selfish human beings, every now and then called "emotional pirates", can prey to your weaknesses. Many instances we fail to understand that at the same time as humans can say hurtful matters to us, we are able to construct ourselves up and make ourselves better with a purpose to be robust towards people who attempt to carry us down. Therefore, as opposed to spending it slow focusing at the negative things human beings let you know, spend time rather addressing any weaknesses you may have and improving on them. Remember, there may be no better comeback than attaining your own personal fulfillment.

-Stay Healthy

In line with the preceding factor, bodily look and health is constantly a point of sensitivity in every person. Popular way of life nowadays comes with a lot of bad things that focus on bodily appearance, which include body shaming. Therefore, one aspect to make your self sense even better and extra confident is to stay a more healthy life-style. A healthy way of life will provide you with extra power and better levels of vanity; resulting in a higher illustration of who you are to the relaxation of the sector.

-Be More Reflective

Learning to pick out selfish humans earlier than they get underneath your pores and skin can virtually assist you cope better when they're around. The motive for that is similar to avoiding contamination; prevention is better than looking to cure. Therefore, being extra reflective on whether the human beings in your life are top allow you to hire coping techniques early; early enough to prevent them absolutely bringing you down.

Here are some signs that let you decide whether or not the character you're with is right for you:

1. When you are with Person X, you sense mild, blissful, and satisfied. During your interactions with them and even once you come across them, you sense energized content. This manner that the man or woman you're with is a person you need to be around, and someone you want to hold a great connection with.

2. Your feelings are continually high-quality whilst you are with Person X. Even though every now and then you may sense tentative, your frame usually feels relaxed and open. If you are feeling this, you likely won't understand the individual that nicely yet. However, this is usually a promising signal which you should invest the time to get to know this person greater. Remember that extra regularly than not, we've got a sure instinctual "alarm machine" that is going off if the individual isn't

wholesome for us. If you sense interested and normally high-quality approximately the man or woman throughout your initial interactions, they'll be well worth making an investment in ultimately.

three. You experience tired or resentful whenever Person X talks to you or seeks out your corporation. Though you can not fully comprehend it yet, this sense of tiredness/exhaustion is typically due to the truth that Person X may be an emotional pirate. It may be that your relationship with this character requires you to expend so much emotional strength listening, comforting, and adjusting to their needs and wants. If you recognize that that is the way you feel after a length of mirrored image, additionally it is a signal that this man or woman is unhealthy for you and your way of life.

-Getting to Know Them

While this will sound like a odd thing to do, some people locate it useful to get to try to get to recognise the person that they'll be at odds with. This is due to the fact maximum of the time, humans have their very own stories and motives why they've come to be the human beings they're these days. It can be beneficial to recognize their stories and their heritage, because it may provide you with more persistence and know-how whilst having to cope with them. It is probably useful to notice that many people who become selfish have come from hard or hard conditions.

-"You Don't Have to Like Each Other to Work With Each Other"

This is genuinely a very beneficial mantra while coping with selfish people on a group, at college, or at paintings. Many instances we fall into a trap by using questioning that we without a doubt can not find a way to work with each other if we don't like every other on a non-public level. The fact is, the alternative is authentic. You can dislike each other on a private level and still find a way to split this from your paintings.

Tell yourself this each time you want to engage or collaborate with someone egocentric. Though their self-concerned behavior might also get at you and annoy you, stop putting additional pressure on your self with the aid of forcing your self to like them. Focus at the venture handy and not on something else. You'll virtually discover your self able to provide optimistic feedback (with out malicious rationale), be more productive, and extra green as a team or duo. Sometimes, you can even find some thing fantastic about them as you pass alongside (they may be virtually knowledgeable about a sure problem, can also have high-quality interest to detail in their output, and many others.)

-Always Have an Exit Strategy

If you know that the character you're assembly up with or having to come across is egocentric, continually set an exit strategy. Don't placed your self in a scenario where you could't leave or where you could't placed the communication on maintain. If you're running or speakme with a egocentric character, you need on the way to take a breather on occasion in order no longer to lose your mood. Therefore, you want to have an strategize and only enter situations in which will now not be too remoted from human beings apart from "Person X".

-Don't Focus on Emotions

Although being with a person selfish could make you feel very terrible and traumatic, one way to control this reaction on your component is to keep away from thinking an emotional manner. For instance, whilst speaking with a person selfish, avoid using emotional phrases like "I feel…", "That's sincerely irritating/stressful/and so on…". Instead, focus on rational mind and phrases, like "I don't think we ought to do that due to the fact…", or "I don't understand if that makes sense to me because….", and the like. If you feel yourself begin to get annoyed, use rational questions or mind to carry you lower back from the edge. When they start getting on your nerves, you may inform yourself "This isn't about me; that is the simply the manner they are".

-Distractions are Key

This is particularly effective for conversations in which you sense just like the different person may be dominating you. Selfish human beings have a tendency to influence the communication simplest to the regions they need to talk about; along with their pastimes and their issues. In order to avoid getting trapped in their emotional "quicksand", make sure you are alert and geared up along with your own subjects to talk approximately. For example, in the event that they start out speakme approximately their dating, be assertive and communicate approximately your personal enjoy as nicely. Then, after inputting your thought, steer the conversations in a very specific direction. For example, if Person X is speakme about their companion having no time for them (which is positive to be the start of a whole rant), you can say some thing like, "Yeah I experienced that too. My boyfriend/girlfriend is a workaholic too. Speaking of labor, did you see the memo they launched approximately the employer holiday?" This will throw them off and optimistically interrupt their goal to speak about their personal troubles to you for the nth time that day, week, or month.

-Limit the Sharing

Selfish humans regularly goal those that have a tendency to be very open and really giving in the direction of others. Though this is not to mention that you need to exchange who you're, it's additionally going to be essential so that you can control this belief in case someone wants to take benefit of you. One manner to do this is to restriction what you proportion. For example, if you helped someone with a trouble in a big way, you don't want to talk about that with potentially selfish humans. Remember that you additionally want to take care of yourself, and part of that is understanding how plenty to percentage and while to share it. Making your self overly available whenever others want you sets unrealistic expectations; ones that you may no longer be able to meet in the long haul.

-Limit the Help

While this could sound like a bad factor, it is also vital that you restriction the help you increase for comparable motives to the factor above. Helping others is a great factor, but you furthermore may need to figure whether your assistance is sincerely needed or whether the character is simply the use of you to do his/her dirty paintings. Helping others remedy the issues they are too lazy to do themselves doesn't definitely remedy whatever; it just allows you to perpetuate the perception that you can be used, and it encourages the cycle of laziness and irresponsibility for the opposite birthday celebration. Therefore, as a way to cope and manipulate the way a egocentric individual treats you and what she or he demands of you, you will also need to set your limits.

-Speak Up, Loud and Clear!

If you locate that a selfish individual you've helped a few times continues on coming returned to you for assist on every little component, then it's time you get up for your self. Remember, this doesn't imply that you need to have a war of words. It's vital that you stay mature and sincere with the aid of sitting down with this individual and having a rational communication with them. Talk to them about very specific instances in which you feel they may have disregarded you and your desires, and the way it made you experience. Let them realize which you additionally have obstacles to what you may provide, and that you are feeling they're asking too much of you. For instance, you may say something like "Hi Joe. I appreciate that you trust me along with your troubles, however when you came to me and requested for my help remaining Friday, I became also truly struggling to make a cut-off date by way of five. I'd find it irresistible in case you requested if I turned Into busy first, and I desire you understand that I additionally have my personal paintings to deal with. Sometimes while you come to me like that, it just makes me sense unappreciated or even every so often taken benefit of. I'm willing to assist from time to time, but I additionally need to be able to admire my obstacles the identical way that I respect you as my colleague." Phrasing it this manner will let them understand that you are criticizing the act, no longer them as people. It may even make clean what you want and want from the character you are dealing with with out offending them.

-Set Boundaries

Some behavioral professionals have said that we are dealt with the way we train human beings to deal with us. This is truely extremely authentic, and we are able to see it in the manner that we have interaction with human beings everyday. Let's take an instance inside the workplace. If we are not able to express that we are uncomfortable with doing activities control, our superiors can also placed us in a role that is heavy on arranging organisation applications. The same idea applies to managing human beings in widespread. You additionally need to claim your identification by using letting people recognise what you're and what you aren't cushty with. A big part of controlling your interactions with selfish human beings is the statement of your barriers, so don't forget about to do this from the get pass.

-An Objective Mind

When you are interacting with someone whom you don't see eye to eye with, it's important which you are available with an goal attitude. Should they method you negatively, don't permit your self be inflamed with a negative spirit as well. You want in an effort to separate yourself from whatever the dating "vibe" is, so being goal is a great manner to defend yourself from emotional pressure and frustration.

-Have a Heart for Understanding

Having a heart for expertise enables cope with stress as it will help you spot egocentric humans no longer as enemies, however as human beings suffering with their very own weaknesses and mistakes. Though they will harm you, it's miles critical to recollect that the proper element to do would be to take the "high" road; this being the choice to help them in place of get returned at them. If they do some thing hurtful toward you, it will likely be simpler to talk behind their back and to get guide from others by gossiping about your enjoy. However, in case you feel which you are in a position to assist prevent the hurtful behavior directed towards you and to stop it from going on to different human beings, you may sit down down and feature a communique with them approximately what they did and the way they made you feel.

-Learn To Walk Away

On the alternative hand, if you feel that you are unable to provide the assist that they need, you need to analyze whilst to walk away. Though all of us have the innate desire to help a person in want, it's important which you additionally realize when it's miles a lost motive. Some human beings are at a point of their lives where they need to help themselves, and that burden should not and can't fall on you.

These are just some of the matters you could do to assist your self cope with selfish human beings.

Chapter 6: The Myth-Of-Agreement

Idiotic Agreements

"Why this 'forcing of sanctioning?' - Because they KNOW their agendas and motivations are askew! They themselves don't believe their own doings and are searching out absolution of duty! They don't want to take a stand, so that they foist it on others to avoid duty by way of petitioning and manipulating others to 'agree.' Agreement, they believe, makes them 'proper.' This is a shortcut to heading off obligation! This is how bullshit-manipulators self-justify and self-delude!"

"If I'm now not in it alone, I'm no longer responsible." Bullshitters con themselves with beliefs like this. If they are able to get in settlement with others, that makes things k, or so they want to believe. Mostly, it's about getting others in agreement with them, due to the fact they want to meet their indulgences. Right and wrong is decided by who has the same opinion with whatever they need to do. This delusion-of-settlement is hard for accurate humans to recognize, mainly the implication that properly and awful are completely flexible, that ethics and requirements are adjusted as convenient.

Avoiding Accountability

"Those who are lazy approximately their non-public ideals, and possibly select to preserve beliefs they recognise are askew and are just undeniable indulgent additionally want their ideals sanctioned, even though uncool. Hence, they're effortlessly manipulated via bullshit-manipulators! One exhibits the other... Associations have their implications."

Avoiding duty is a massive purpose and motivation at the back of a good deal the bullshitter does. If they're accountable, then they can be held responsible, an eventuality they keep away from at all fees. Everything with them is a lie, responsibility is related to exposure, their big worry.

They want to unfold the risk, and prefer to associate with individuals who also like doing this. They can reinforce every other. Not simply in spreading threat, but in at the same time helping indulgences, favored ideals, and questioning. An vintage announcing as it should be adapted to apply to this bullshit association of comfort: "Birds of a feather lie collectively."

Inadvertent Condoning

"Bullshitter-manipulators bank on oldsters no longer looking to make the extra effort required to deal with the uncomfortable and awkward truths. And it is how folks get manipulated and duped, and are complicit to the egregious acts of bullshitters. Condoning bullshit, however subtle, isn't an choice! Complicity isn't an alternative!"

We can agree without agreeing, via now not disagreeing. Yes, it seems difficult at first, but our lack of disagreement is taken by using the bullshitter as settlement. They will act and behave as if we agreed. A clever manipulative trick. Or as a minimum they like to suppose so. They leverage our dislike and avoidance of disagreement, awkwardness, and uncomfortableness to strain us with our own crappiness into "letting it be."

We assume we're deciding on the lesser of the evils, but we're not. Letting cancer alone while it starts, is a extreme movement with extreme consequences. We can't permit bullshit to be condoned, no matter how inadvertently. We turn out to be answerable for what it results in. Seldom does it remember in the immediately, but continually it topics inside the lengthy-time period.

Crappy Conscience

"Bullshitters will go to first rate lengths to govern and force a public belief of agreement in an try and assuage a responsible conscience and dented ego."

This manipulation of their own moral sense is a fascinating self-bullshit. Why does it work for the bullshitter? Because they're hollow interior. Because their lives are made of figment and now not real getting to know and growing, no longer acquiring a actual and unbiased self, they're hole. They tackle whatever is the triumphing "have to." They adapt to anything they think is currently "cool" or "in," and anything they trust will get them approval and interest.

That's their consciousness. All that subjects is that "they," maximum of their circle or community, or maybe people in popular, trust and experience regardless of the bullshitter has taken on as their personal. These deceivers are moral chameleons, chameleons of conscience. Whatever works, anything is convenient. They're chameleons with a special trick: They change the environment to healthy the coloration they need to expose. When that color is the color of an erased conscience, they will visit super lengths to manufacture settlement from sufficient to allow them to apply their myth-of-settlement. "If sufficient agree, then it's okay."

"Overriding conscience is a sluggish suicide of self. Conscience can not be absolved with bullshit."

One could assume bullshitters and in particular BMNs, don't have a judgment of right and wrong, however they do. It's precisely because they do have a few little bit of conscience that they hotel to lies. Deception is the duvet-up, the obfuscation, they need to hide themselves from their moral sense. It's this that makes bullshitters so terrible. They recognize what they do is wrong. Yet they do it anyway.

They transgress towards themselves because they actually insist on their indulgences. They refuse to give these up, believing that doing so makes them "losers" and "inferior." So thoroughly enslaved are they by way of their root mis-beliefs, it reasons them to head towards themselves, resulting in perpetual distress and no hope of real happiness, leaving them to resort to bullshit happiness.

Ethical Emptiness

"The mis-perception that settlement equates rightness cannot be used to control the absolution of corrupt moral sense. The root notion of the conformity mind-set is that 'if others do it, it should be okay,' and for that reason it's a validation, is a fantasy. Both goodness and crappiness want to be determined on their own deserves. Else we turn out to be with the lowest commonplace denominator."

The crime of bullshit in popular, the cancer of bullshit, lies on this consistent knocking down of the whole thing. Lower and lower, till we're all within the shitpile with the bullshitter, until we're all lower than them, till there are not any requirements, no ethics. Until we're at that degree of emptiness and indulgence where the bullshitter resides and where they're cushty. Indulgence continuously drags us down into an area wherein duty and ethics, standards and values, and some thing which requires some degree of attempt that's now not indulging infantile dreams doesn't exist.

When we recognize that the bullshitter psychology hasn't matured beyond that childish degree of wanting whatever it desires regardless of what, then an awful lot turns into clean. They've discovered that tons of what they want isn't k, but they've also discovered they are able to control their wants and desires into being ok, if they are able to get others to believe them. Bullshitters love the myth-of-settlement, because it permits them.

Corrupting Justification

"Legitimacy and validation, when not inherently decided by way of standards consisting of ethics, good judgment, and motive, are then 'confirmed' with the aid of exchange method which includes like-minded agreement and affiliation, which might be subtly leveraged to validate, pushing the belief that after others accept as true with it, it ought to be proper. If others validate it, it ought to be so. It's a deception of mutually reinforcing private dishonesty."

The usefulness of the myth-of-agreement works both methods. Those they involve also advantage from this usefulness. Often these are clearly desirable humans, however ones that for something motive end up constant on a selected time table that's important to them.

Sadly, they will compromise their goodness and their ethics to gain their schedule, justifying those transgressions of judgment of right and wrong with that insidious distortion: "The quit justifies the manner."

Unfortunately, this belief simply enables spread corruption and unavoidably leads to a stained result, not to mention the complications and problems now because of those "method." Solving one trouble at the fee of creating others isn't any answer at all. Polluting the arena to smooth up an island is hardly beneficial. Good human beings often succumb to bullshit common sense once they end up immersed in a few attention or other they consider in. Whenever we compromise our ethics, we input into bullshit, a slippery slope, which simplest ends in the shitpile.

"There's a set dynamic at play that is insidious, corrupt, and subtle while the implied consent and validation of bullshit are willingly bought into."

Good humans are also liable to the myth-of-settlement. They very a good deal can fall prey to this belief that "if all people thinks it's appropriate, it's far." All way of horrors in records have been perpetrated in the call of this delusion. The concept that settlement constitutes rightness or goodness is just bullshit. If we look at superstitions we speedy see the lie and nonsense of this belief.

Vacuous Validity

"Implied agreement and approval fosters the notion of validity whilst there's none. 'If others consider me, I must be right.'"

The difficulty with this specific bullshit perception is that in terms of figuring out fact, rightness, and goodness, we're honestly on our very own. A responsibility few are willing to undertake. Lest we're also organized to be bullshitters, but limited, we need to be inclined to stand alone when it comes to the responsibilities of being an excellent and first rate man or woman.

We ought to make the ones hard selections for ourselves. Right or wrong, we ought to make the choice, we must take the obligation, and we truely have to do our great. It's all we will do. We have help, we most effective ought to have a look at the bullshitter and notice their depressing hole corrupt lives and selves to warn us of the risks and detriments of not being our own individual. The bullshitter is totally corrupted due to their refusal to be a actual person.

"Joiners, followers, and 'fans' who additionally have compromised methods, beliefs, and agendas are really, with the aid of affiliation, deemed to validate wilful indulgences, and therefore at the same time enhance a lack of ethics. The soliciting of what are actually accomplices is an try to legitimise unsubstantiated attitudes, behaviours, and beliefs."

If we observe bullshitters who have a "following," who've admirers and sycophants, we see a unhappy institution. Toadies and spineless panderers who have not anything are not anything, who're desperate for any crumb. A very well odious situation. When looking at this from the outdoor, we surely see its corruption, and how we want not anything in any respect to do with such a crowd, and the concept of being part of it's miles beyond terrible.

We should take into account that whenever we bullshit, even in small methods, ways we suppose are insignificant, we're in truth joining any such organization, a collection that pollutes the arena. Just because we're no longer truly in a specific circle doesn't suggest we're now not in a larger less well defined association. If we bullshit ourselves, even a bit, we be a part of that greater gang of defilement.

If we care approximately our international, how, just how, will we justify polluting it with bullshit?

Co-opting Complicity

Leveraging Social Awkwardness

"Bullshit-manipulator-narcissists flip indulgence into a manner-of-being! Public settlement or condonance of indulging is a slippery slope. This is how allegiance gets co-opted, how bullshit entanglements and groupings come into being: by way of co-opting the goodness of typically right humans and turning it into complicity."

Indulging their desire to be visible as "high-quality" and "pleasant" and "cool" is of essential significance to the BMN. They're acutely privy to all of the nuance worried with this indulgence. So intimately familiar are they with all of the ins and outs of look, image, and the approval-disapproval of others that they're capable of use and control this understanding innately. They will fully make the most the choice of accurate human beings to not motive unpleasantness, to no longer be rude, to not make a scene and to now not "appearance terrible." These are our indulgences. Yes, to a significantly lesser diploma, however the BMN will take advantage of and use them without qualm.

Our desire to be Good, and to as a consequence supply the advantage of the doubt, to agree with, to not think sick of others, to not be unpleasant, and comparable, are all turned on us. If we're wimpy and "susceptible," refusing to stand up for ourselves or to call BS when it is egregious or in any other case fail to do what's proper, in spite of being ugly, we best have ourselves accountable if our indulgence is used in opposition to us. The worst of it's miles we emerge as complicit within the unethical doings of the BMN.

"Bullshit can't continue to exist on its own. It requires complicity of a few type."

For instance, you and your associate are in a set social setting with a BMN whom you both realize, but the rest of these gift do no longer. Someone mentions a need for assistance of some kind. The BMN pipes up and presents a bullshit photo of how they can be of help. You and your companion realize that is garbage, but pronouncing something will significantly embarrass your BMN "buddy" or should purpose an issue and a "scene." So you keep silent and let it run its course.

The BMN knows you're in all likelihood to no longer say some thing, and your lack of competition or disagreement can be used by them, via subtle implication to lend support to their bullshit self-merchandising. The person at the receiving quit who has no way of understanding as a result believes the BMN, as there's no reason now not to. They take your non-opposition as settlement or support for the BMN and their claims. It's all harmless at the floor. The individual inquiring for help has no concept of what is definitely taking place and will handiest find out later, while it is too overdue.

"There's no goodness in appeasement, as it's definitely beside the point tolerance. A mis-perception we cannot find the money for."

Problem is, we're now complicit in embroiling that individual with the bullshit of the BMN. Unfortunately, BMNs continually overestimate their abilities, biting off way beyond realistic objectives. They just like the photo, status, and appearance of being capable even beyond what their bullshit guarantees, however can seldom supply. Always, while failing to live as much as their hype, they use bullshit to get them out of hassle, blaming the whole thing else but themselves.

Nonetheless, the person at the receiving end has had their time or money wasted. The worst part of this is that we're entirely complicit via our non-movement. The quicker we realize we are able to't always simply say not anything to avoid capability unpleasantness, the earlier we enable ourselves to act. Because our goodness will even no longer allow us to be complicit. We virtually need to understand and end up aware of this result. As right human beings, it then turns into our moral obligation to now not be complicit!

Implied Endorsement

"The manipulation of my consent and tremendous interaction is being compelled from me, and that is simply wrong! Bad! This forcing of my positivity is to sanction the bullshit-manipulator's being, that's sincerely sanctioning their manipulation, their crappiness, their lack of ethics and integrity. This is stealing my goodness, impinging on my positivity! This is how bullshit-manipulator-narcissists scouse borrow freedom! 'I accept and admire your difference; simply don't pressure and manage me into sanctioning it!' We had been by no means pals, so the agenda to be 'friends' and seem 'pleasant' is suspect! The coercion of my positive interplay for incorrect-motivation is totally unethical!"

BMNs cross the strains of normal well mannered interaction. They will engineer compelled agreements thru informal harmless seeming feedback like: "I'm sure you will all agree." Or the usage of a person's name intentionally, as in: "I'm certain Joe will agree," then easily shifting on. This co-opted help is gained in passing and in no way targeted on without delay. The bullshitter directs attention through emphasis elsewhere, obscuring that tacit endorsement, making it hard for us to not go together with this diffused manipulation and thereby securing that every one-critical implied substantiation.

What they're asking agreement to is typically so undefined, it's hard to object. Likewise, they may use our popular goodness to, by means of implication, aid them. They can assume a "friendship" primarily based on not anything greater than our positivity and friendliness. Overstepping the bounds of ordinary well mannered interaction to pressure an implied sanctioning in their bullshit, and as a consequence via implication, of their being and their agendas, as their bullshit is commonly some type of self-merchandising.

It's a sneaky trick, due to the fact how will we item? If we are saying, "Hey, we are not friends yet, I haven't long gone that far," then we're the ones who appear petty and ridiculous. Likely the BMN will simply flip round and say some thing like, "What makes you suspect we're? That's a chunk presumptuous," consequently turning the tables on us.

The only manner to address that is to learn how to realise the bullshitters and BMNs, and thru being aware, prevent such actions via withholding our positivity and friendliness until we're sure they might not be abused and misused. All we really want is merely to withhold for even a few seconds, to surely no longer make our perceptions and interactions with others automated. Once our positivity, and thus our implied approval is given, it is hard to take again.

A unique strategy to the above instance, when the bullshitter claims agreement on our behalf, would be a simple polite shake of the head or a impartial, "Um, no." Just that is sufficient to direct emphasis on their ploy, collapsing all their trickery and bullshit. The implications of our easy motion are at once apparent. The bullshitter now is aware of we realize, making us risky to use as a compelled best friend. Once is normally enough, because the bullshitter is careful to not threat exposure. A threat they in no way take until they really ought to.

Once they realize we see their sport and won't play along, they may look some other place for unaware allies to co-opt. If the Joe isn't us and would not word or is unaware of their inadvertent complicity, we can nonetheless derail the bullshit with some thing like "Do you, Joe?"

Simple non-reputation and non-settlement derails inadvertent complicity; going a long manner toward thwarting manipulated entanglement into bullshit.

Forced Friendliness

"Bullshit-manipulators coerce our politeness, sneakily embroiling us in a non-existent dating or settlement. It's about forcing an interplay! Being privy to this manipulation is key."

As Murphy said in certainly one of his different laws, "It's simpler to get into things than to get out." We get tricked by the seeming friendliness and appeal of the BMN. If we take those extra few seconds to appearance deeper, to invite, "What's the intent here?" we commonly get a clue that something isn't because it seems. This pause is all we need to prevent interacting in methods with a purpose to lead us off beam.

For exact human beings, this isn't smooth, as we want for all people to be properly and satisfactory. We want there are no horrific people, we want for goodness and positivity. In the actual global, attention is the problem. We may be properly, and excellent, and fine, AND aware, all on the equal time. We without a doubt need to construct that pause and that discernment into our habitual interactions and behaviours.

"Bullshit-manipulator-narcissists are insistent on getting their foot in the door! Any door! Just pronouncing hello or hi may be a manipulation of our goodness. This hi-jacking of our goodness is a segway right into a relationship that one doesn't necessarily want to be a part of."

It's now not clean to reply to acknowledged BMNs whilst we meet them out inside the international. They will greet us with a splendid friendliness like we're long-time near friends.

Especially if we've come to understand what precisely they are, and we realize they're no longer nice and suitable human beings. Our instinct and habit is to reply to friendliness with friendliness.

But with a recognised BMN we need to check that impulse, responding with neutrality instead. Responding with an attention that transmits, "I understand what you're and need no a part of it, thanks." Typically, bullshitters fear focus. It's their Kryptonite. Awareness of bullshit displays what is taking place, and bullshit can't thrive while it's manifestly bullshit; then it is just lame.

"We like to agree with that our non-specific actions don't make us complicit, however they do! We're simply as answerable for our non-moves as our actions. Inadvertent complicity thru irresponsible inattention and state of being inactive has detrimental outcomes not with no trouble obvious. We tend to believe that complicity is simplest an overt and planned movement, however this isn't the case."

Non-movement is a effective lever for the bullshitter. If we don't item or explicit overt confrontation, we're deemed to agree. We're as a consequence robotically made complicit. The leverage used is that we do not need to head around being unpleasant.

There are many methods to disagree without simply pronouncing anything, and those are the most effective while coping with bullshit. We simply have to reveal that we don't agree, we do not should spell it out or say why. For many this is probably tough, but if we do not, we grow to be complicit, allowing bullshitters to get away with their bullshit.

Too Much Effort

"The willingness of excellent oldsters to be deceived because of their reluctance to suppose matters via, their preference for a quick and easy solution, and to vicinity responsibility on a person else and keep away from the stresses of independent wondering makes them complicit. Their willingness to accept as true with self belief leads them deeply off target. Confidence is not enough."

Complicity comes in lots of forms. Our laziness, our reluctance to take a stand, our unwillingness to "get involved," our resistance to considering matters, to deal with a "heavy" subject matter, and our dislike of managing unsightly truths all make us complicit. We like to think we keep away from related to ourselves with the unpleasant and the bad, but that avoidance is exactly what makes us complicit, because we allow it to exist, to preserve, to hold on.

If we consider bullshit as an epidemic, as an infectious sickness, it changes matters drastically. Especially in terms of the BMN. Their narcissism takes non-resistance as agreement, as a consequence they take our non-action as condoning them. A seriously dangerous and probably disastrous route we're part of placing them on.

Bullshit is the start. Unchecked and affirmed delusion permits all their rotten dispositions and might lead to critically terrible and criminal behaviour, especially once they begin to sense invulnerable.

"It takes much less electricity and is less difficult and faster to indulge and appease bullshit than to confront or address it. There's a social conference to placate, appease, and condone bullshit to facilitate 'first-class' interaction."

If we but think matters via a piece in relation to bullshit, we fast see it's no longer a simple difficulty, now not a not anything problem, but a extreme problem hidden within the apparently non-severe, harmless, and trivial. Pretence hides all styles of ills, and this is what makes it so risky, specifically because it's through this cover that our complicity is stolen. Much like cancer grows as it fools our immune machine, so bullshit eats at goodness.

Mass Mis-Beliefs

"The externally-stimulated-character, the bullshitter-narcissist, is based at the fake premise that communally supported behaviour is legitimate, however it's not, because a lot behaviour is commonly only supported to avoid war."

The bullshitter likes convenient ideals together with: "But if all of us does it, it must be k" or, "If everybody is of the same opinion, it ought to be proper." Both of those are false. We can take a look at records and superstitions to look how fake they're. These beliefs are how our complicity is hijacked.

If we're taken to be in settlement due to the fact we are saying not anything, because we do not item or disagree, we're one of these hundreds that makes that false belief appear real and valid. We become a part of the hassle, a part of the mis-belief. We're complicit.

It's precisely this which lets in terrible politicians and other societal ills to exist. It's a particular hassle in terms of bullshitters, due to the fact they're completely aware of this mechanism and actively use it to in addition their bullshit with the aid of obtaining a seeming average fashionable settlement, and consequently, their bullshit comes to be taken as real, without a doubt because no one had the gumption, braveness, nor ethics to item and disagree. They recognise maximum people don't like to go against the crowd, no matter how actual and obvious the truth might be.

"If you are inclined to trust anything fits your motive with out substantiation or validation, you deserve to be manipulated."

Just so. If we do not anything, we're complicit. And responsible.

Dealing with Inconvenience

Unpleasant Truth

"I actually have discovered, whilst we take the time to reply the atypical and strange, every so often inconvenient questions, which we can't keep away from if we're honest, we come to that point in which we will honestly translate them into utilisable recognition."

Most frequently that query is as easy as, "What's taking place?" We often ask this query, but just leave it there. It's an expression and acknowledgement by way of us that something isn't precisely proper. Typically, we do not appearance deeper.

If we move similarly and actually exercise session and consider what's clearly going on, we get to peer the fullness of the scenario. This may not be convenient or pretty. It's higher to recognize beforehand when there's nevertheless possibility to deal with matters than leaving it to fester and complicate, and eventually reason us a lot more problem and trouble.

"Indulgent recoil-fests and untrustworthy reports permit one to act on that awareness if we pay interest and research. Awareness brings with it responsibility. Awareness with out application is incomprehensible."

A powerful quote which has an awful lot to it. If we're cringing or embarrassed or uncomfortable or in any manner put out by way of a person's behaviour or phrases, it's a clear warning. If we, as most humans do, cover this up, refuse to pay attention, and in any other case disguise from awkwardness, we handiest permit the bullshitter, mainly when they purpose to manipulate us.

They assume our aversion to unpleasantness and deliberately create situations that leverage our reluctance to deal with the awkward and uncomfortable. They recognise they can say and do all way of outrageousness, and we won't item or call them out due to the fact we're frightened of unpleasantness or absolutely don't want to be inconvenienced.

That intended convenience is a huge rate to pay for the entanglement and complicity via this assist of the bullshit. If we don't display in some manner that we're not in support, bullshitters will use our silence, evasion, and non-objection as settlement. They will do that actively.

Unfortunately there are instances we simply have to chunk the bullet, suck it up, and deal with that inconvenience, awkwardness, and unpleasantness. Even sometimes beginning it. If we do not, we are able to for all time thereafter be held hostage by our wimpiness and weak spot. We do not must make a scene or do anything drastic. We merely need to allow our function be known.

We can do this quietly, softly, with out fuss. Often we can show wherein we're at simply with our cognizance, posture, or expression. A disapproving look seen by using all can forestall a bullshitter most correctly. We simply ought to have simply that little bit of courage, decency, and ethics to now not allow the infection of bullshit to spread. Bullshit is a disease of negativity, no matter how much it may be disguised in apparent "friendliness" and other meant high-quality disguises. It's now not cool, or best, or harmless. Quite the alternative.

"It takes all types to make up the ecosystem. Rotten apples belong in the compost - it's beside the point to have them at your dinner table."

Acknowledging Ignorance

"The acknowledgement of lack of expertise is a need - it is a part of existence. Without this simple recognition, studying is near not possible."

An inconvenient fact the bullshitter avoids with all of their being is the acknowledgement in their own lack of understanding and nincompoopery. It's some thing all of us have, regardless of how a whole lot we may think otherwise. This is in reality a fact. Most people realize this and receive it as part of being human, making efforts to cope with this reality, getting to know and developing, and in this way enhancing ourselves.

The bullshitter really refuses to deal with their lack of expertise and foolishness. A truth it is a horror to them, to be avoided in any respect prices. They refuse to apply the necessary efforts most people make to remedy this situation. It's their refusal and avoidance of this fact of lifestyles that leads them to motel to bullshit. They use deception to now not handiest cowl the truth of what they're, however also use their myth as a substitute for learning, inside the procedure bullshitting themselves that they're growing.

This is an impossibility. An inconvenient truth they in turn also refuse to stand, and thereby create a existence which has no wish truly. They stay all the time ignorant and incompetent, silly and silly. They can't truely ever be anything, as their entire being is founded on this idiotic concept that they are able to cheat their way into being something. They consider that definitely being able to fool others is sufficient.

It isn't always, and the most inconvenient of all of the truths is that they can never idiot themselves, no matter how hard they are trying. In the end they constantly realize the real reality about themselves, that they're an empty nothing. What a rate to pay, excited by the "benefit" of heading off a simple reality of lifestyles that applies to us all. Sad.

"The mere acquisition of statistics is neither mastering nor intelligence."

The inconvenience of mastering doesn't appeal to the bullshitter in the least. Neither does the

131

inconvenience of not being splendid smart. Instead of creating real efforts to address those truths, they want to cheat their manner to simulating some kind of appearance of intelligence and mastering. One of the methods they try this is thru repeating and regurgitating records they've picked up.

In unique, bullshitters will repeat and "re-promote" what's inspired them. So arrogant and ego-centric are they, that they simply assume if they didn't realize, then no person else did either. They will then take this newfound know-how and use it to try to provoke others, assuming all people else would be equally inspired. They do not recognise simply how ignorant they're relative to others, because of their existence of lying to themselves about how an awful lot they realize.

It's an inconvenient fact that their very efforts to try to appear informed and shrewd are completely counterproductive, stressful the very fact they're trying to cover up. Even more charming is how they may grasp onto something a person stated, and if it got here out impressively and sounded smart or wise, or in a few manner vital, they may certainly thieve, reproduction, and repeat what they heard without really even expertise what they're saying. Often they'll use this borrowed facts and words in a context that's utterly irrelevant, exposing their utter ignorance, foolishness, stupidity, and bullshit.

Usually though, those who know what has came about genuinely record the implications away, making the appropriate reassessment of the counterfeiter. So caught up is the bullshitter in the idea that they're "selling" themselves as smart or clever etc., that they don't realize the counterproductive implications of this ridiculous form of deceit. If it wasn't so tragic, it'd be hilarious, and often is.

"The preposterous can take place, does occur, has took place, is taking place!"

Implications

"We cannot handiest awareness on convenient truths; we need to pay equal interest to the inconvenient."

133

Our own nonsense, however small, has huge consequences when interacting with bullshitters. Especially our dislike of inconvenient truths. They will exploit this reluctance to deal with those inconvenient, but real, ugly realities by means of leveraging our unwillingness to call them on their rubbish. Or they will manage us, understanding we avoid confrontation. There are many methods our personal foolishness causes us hassle. BMNs will use anything they can to in addition their agendas.

What prevents us from coping with manipulators appropriately? Usually it's surely our reluctance to make that little bit of more attempt. Isn't this short-sightedness of our very own, BS of our personal? It is. If we desire to cope with bullshit, we have to permit move of our personal silliness, however small, otherwise the charge we pay for that crappiness may be tremendously high.

Malignant Manipulation

Manipulating Niceness

"The bullshit-manipulator's M.O. Is to exploit one's loves and connections, and one's preference to no longer pressure and cause hassle for others. To no longer motive a scene, to play the sport of being friendly, best, and considerate - the whole thing they're no longer! Yet purport to be. They care most effective approximately their own wishes. The entire schedule is to try pulling one right down to seem better by way of assessment, and for this reason feed their narcissism."

The first step in an interaction for a bullshit-manipulator-narcissist is determining their most important and nearly instinctual goal which is to determine whether or not their con is running, has labored. If the recipient buys the bullshit, they're dupes and suitable applicants as "buddies," and consequently effortlessly dealt with, coerced, manipulated, and used for all their resources, connections and popularity.

These "buddies" are actually "owned" by means of the BMN and are called upon for help, help, and commiseration at every whim to preserve their compliance as serfs to the bullshit-manipulator-narcissist.

Worse Than

"Bullshit-manipulators look to hold their energetics and entanglements to get their way and piss on a situation, marking it as territory just to justify their being and persona. They'll force the illusion of 'friendliness' or being a terrific recreation. They exploit what's essential to others and use that to control and take advantage of goodness. Anytime one has an attachment to some thing, it could be exploited. However, if one cares about ethics first and essential, all other affections are secondary, and it's easy to stroll away."

The bullshit-manipulator-narcissist is extraordinarily resentful of all of us whom they understand as "higher-than" them. Their psychologies are deeply threatened via easy perceptions like, "wow, here's an truly glad man or woman!" The comparative-mind-set of the BMN has to strive destroying what it believes is critique and unfavorable reflection, even though most effective by way of implication.

They will try this pull-down with each tactic of their arsenal, beginning subtly at first, with passive-aggressive movements, regularly ramping up their efforts in the event that they don't acquire success, subsequently ending with full-blown bullying and outright blatant negativity. If possible, they prefer to manipulate their manner to a few sort of relative "betterness."

This they will do by attempting to set up a shape of control, be it financial, home, or social. This dominance can manifest through determining who the opposite's buddies are for them, and what they're "allowed" to do, or different such absurdities. As lengthy as the BMN feels someone is dependent on them in a few manner, they are able to bullshit themselves they're "superior."

"The wall-of-strength that bullshitters foist is an emotional, active, and psychological entanglement, which is foisted to collect 'relative status,' via underhanded way, which includes: 'higher-than,' 'more in-price,' 'smarter-than,' 'greater superior,' 'denigrating,' 'greater seductive,' 'invasive,' 'greater attractive,' 'demeaning,' 'greater hip,' 'derogatory,' 'more cool,' 'dominant,' 'intrusive,' 'ingratiating,' and so on. And so forth. Essentially, an try to establish top-dog popularity or, failing that, implied approval and agreement. Tacit condoning makes you the implied bottom-canine for this form of psychology. And as a consequence relative superiority is finagled."

The bullshit-manipulator-narcissist coerces desirable people to "open the door" via bullying, permitting them to plunder, take, use, and abuse something they may. They're corrupters and polluters of environments. Once they've tainted a state of affairs, a unfastened-for-all is created for different parasites, enabling nefarious dealings and a feeding from their scraps. In the process, glorifying the BMN as benefactors. They revel in flattening people and places, relishing corrosion via their indulgence, for that reason scary the bottom not unusual denominator in others.

Egregious Association

"The wall-of-electricity bullshitters impose exploits loss of confrontation, that is then taken as agreement, although it's not! The loss of competition is contorted and manipulated into support, which we're now party to, despite the fact that we do not honestly agree!"

The bullshit-manipulator-narcissist needs control and "possession" of people and matters within the guise of being "pals." Maintaining manage of the opposite individual and anything assets they may have by way of "assisting," flattery, solicitations, and apparently benign "invites." They're infiltrators and polluters of organizations, homes, individuals, and communities at big. Association with the BMN has a adverse effect.

Anyone who's aware and savvy sufficient to see thru the bullshit doesn't need to be associated with nefarious individuals who disguise themselves as "first-class" and "friendly." Furthermore, individuals who do partner with the BMN prove themselves to be fools, and now not well worth the hazard, final opportunities due to infection with the aid of affiliation.

Pollution can't show up if doorways aren't opened, and parents aren't amenable to bullshit and skewed agendas. Discernment is required regarding who we permit into our houses, hearts, and businesses, otherwise we allow ourselves to be manipulated thru our simple however naive friendliness.

"The cause-distortion bullshitter's leverage is an emotional, lively, and mental entanglement foisted upon others to engineer complicit agreements the use of overt lack of disagreements. A manipulative bullying which abuses people's goodness, politeness, and courtesy. Why do bullshitters impose this power round their middle of distortion? Because it calls for counter-strength to interrupt thru the purported 'innocuous' reason and get to the underlying crappiness. It's extra expedient in strength expenditure terms to simply be herded with the triumphing imposition than it's far to resist."

Depths of Discernment

Conspirators

"Bullshit is a conspiracy."

We're a part of the conspiracy without even completely realising. Or perhaps we do. Whenever we pander to bullshit, on every occasion we permit it to propagate thru our inactions and non-actions, every time we turn a blind-eye, every time we smile and nod in response to gross fake bullshit, we end up a part of the conspiracy. A conspiracy we're being asked to condone by means of implication.

"It's no longer simply what bullshit-manipulators say; it's all inside the theatre in their eyes, smile, cognizance, mind-set, walk, speak, voice, script, chuckle, strength, posture, hand gestures, face projection, hair, apparel. Etcetera."

Bullshitters also conspire with every different. Not directly, instead subtly, by way of implication. They feed each other's delusions with together reinforcing agreements and the arrival of offering advantage due to their contortions.

For example, A has something B needs, who schmoozes A to get it, believing as is their dependancy, "this is the manner it's accomplished." A, in this example, has to deliver the benefit anyway. B just happens to be available, and A, also being a bullshitter, seizes at the possibility to make B think they're giving out the advantage because of B's manipulations, making them sense their efforts paid off. A in turn receives the "gain" of making B beholden to them. Thus they input their conspiracy of falsehood. Of course the moment neither desires the other, they'll drop them immediately. Bullshit conspirators haven't any loyalty.

Ugly Truths

"We best call it bullshit due to the fact we're uncomfortable and awkward dealing with the innate deception and underlying ugliness of those 'non-planned' machinations."

Discernment is unfortunately now not usually pretty nor excellent. If we're to avoid being inadvertent conspirators in the proliferation of deception which abounds nowadays, we want to cope with that unpleasantness. This doesn't imply we need to confront or "name out" each bullshitter we come upon. We needn't necessarily even deal with any of them.

What we do want to stand are our internal perceptions. We need to move wherein our discernment leads us. Not shying away from uncomfortable truths. Yes, the side impact is that we carry the crap of bullshit into our global, however it's higher to peer the shit and understand it's there than step in it.

Deliberate Motives

"Bullshit is extra than exaggeration; it's deeper, deliberate, deceitful... An unsightly lying due to the fact the intent is to lie to!"

In our normal lives, we encounter bullshit, we know such persons, however generally don't pay it a good deal mind. "It's just nonsense." If we think about it, how did that "nonsense" manifest? Randomly? No, alas not. It didn't "simply pop out."

With some attention, we fast see there needed to be some notion behind that falseness; now not the unique phrases perhaps, but the intent and the time table. Why exactly are they placing out what isn't? This is the query to ask. What's the purpose behind it? Now we get somewhere. Through this we come to recognize that the garbage isn't idle nor mere happenstance. Deceit, or manipulation, these motivations are ever near. There's an time table and an cause to provide the self as something aside from what it's far. Deception is mendacity, commonly simply oblique mendacity, however nonetheless lying.

144

Manipulation is likewise oblique lying, and worse, it's abuse.

"Covert arrogance... Timid bullying... Deceptions which we must be aware about. Hence the necessity for discernment."

If we ask ourselves, "If I had been to bullshit, what might be my reason? What would be behind it?" Coming at the rationale from the opposite facet quickly lets in us to see what's worried. Can we sincerely simply push falsehood for no cause? Not probably. Behind the deceptions are real reasons, and those motives aren't first-rate.

If we strip away the deception of our very own refusal to cope with deceit and spot it for what it surely is, we see the horrific intents and motivations behind the pretence. To willingly and knowingly lie to others for a few advantage is not excellent. There's not anything benign approximately this, no matter how a whole lot the bullshitter attempts to convince us in any other case.

"Some of the worst bullies cover in the back of a facade of timidity. A timid bully is still a bully; simply a disguised bully!"

The benefits of squarely facing the ugly realities underlying bullshit live in the cognizance we gain, allowing us to discern what's certainly occurring. Further knowledge of the deceptions and manipulations lie in the implications. What does it say approximately someone when they deliberately employ abuse and deceit? Implications with regards to bullshitters aren't quality inside the least.

To intentionally lie to and control others way a rottenness of being, it means bullshitters aren't top people. This they understand. It's one of the reasons for the distortions in the first vicinity. Their aim is to hide and cowl-up this awful truth. Why they take incredible pains to give themselves as "pleasant," even timid or shy, or a few other contrived disguise. Discernment is asking past the floor, past what's offered, looking at what lies in the back of, at what's definitely occurring.

Arrogance

"Arrogance is often well disguised, covert, and diffused. Yet we generally tend to accept as true with it handiest exists in overt form."

A distinguishing element of bullshitters is their very own recognition of the not-niceness of what they do. They understand their actions aren't proper, they know they're dishonest. They know they're stealing from others, stealing our goodwill and effective strength. If what they get from us is a end result of falsehood, it's stealing. Because they so surely know what they're honestly doing is unjustifiable, they visit excellent pains to hide and disguise, obfuscate and distract. A vital necessity of deception.

"Mis-perceiving conceitedness for confidence, and self belief for appropriate intention, has devastating consequence."

One of our most dangerous mis-perceptions of a BMN occurs when they could correctly sell their arrogance as confidence. Then, thru the self assurance they convince us they have excellent intentions, and are acting in our interest. But this isn't feasible for them. Their psychologies absolutely gained't permit authentic selflessness.

No depend how a whole lot their moves can also appear directed in the direction of the good of others, at bottom there's always some non-public time table that's fundamental. It can also so take place that others derive superb benefit, however this won't be to the BMN's liking, due to the fact they always need to be the one who blessings the maximum. The best time they are able to bear to see others benefit is once they're reaping rewards plenty greater. Always that evaluation and hierarchy is present. When we see apparent advantage from a BMN, it's time to be mainly cautious.

Strategic Neutrality

"There's actually no desirable motive for involvement, 'friendship,' or the appearance of 'friendliness' with a bullshitter. A modicum of civility is a generosity which might be suitable if not coerced, as there's no actual interest from them in 'friendship' or touching on, apart from the schedule of appearances, self-merchandising, and relative superiority. There's no upside to interacting. All it does is serve to keep their photo-facade. Life is for living, for sincerity, for integrity, for realness, for proper genuineness. Faking goodness is moronic!"

Interacting with a regarded bullshitter, mainly a BMN, may be hard. A undertaking requiring the software of discernment. If we behave and react consistent with our natural dispositions and conduct of goodness, responding with friendliness, all we accomplish is legitimising the bullshitter. Or worse, we in all likelihood will want to deal with entanglement. We also don't need to be outright unfriendly or impolite, even though it is probably warranted. This is going against our grain. Limiting our interactions and responses to the naked minimum and keeping a very impartial mindset works nicely.

Yes, there are times when open unfriendliness is probably referred to as for, if the terrible moves of a bullshitter are blatant and simple. This is rare, as they take first rate pains to "cowl" their doings, by no means opening themselves to definitive censure. Always everything with them is unclear. But, our discernment and expertise lets in us to peer exactly what they're, and what they're as much as. "Proving" this in a technical feel is hard. Thus, if we're overtly adverse we run the risk of the bullshitter going on the counter-offensive. When we're not gift, they can, and will, distort topics in their favour, using our open hostility as "proof" the fault lies with us. Typical bullshit approaches.

Our neutral stance, no longer friendly and not unfriendly, is robust when it comes to bullshitters and BMNs. Much in their distortion and manipulation depends on implication. Our loss of pleasant response to their common pressured friendliness is by way of implication an indictment of them. We also can't be faulted for any intended unreasonable or illogical behaviour. Thus, our neutrality is a effective non-wonderful mirrored image on them, particularly if that is accomplished within the organization of others. Those who be aware will see something is amiss and placed two and collectively, the very result the bullshitter fears most. Public opinion and approval is vitally vital to them. They can't easily assault an unbiased stance, with out it being obvious they've an agenda, and with out them "looking bad." We can use their personal nonsense to cope with them.

Neutrality is a effective tool in our arsenal when dealing with bullshit. We might also accept as true with we want to take a robust stand, and we do. When it comes to managing those snakes and fakes, they will use something that is critical to us as a lever for manipulation. Any sturdy emotion lets them recognize in which they could push our buttons, in which they can pressure us, and therefore how they could manipulate us. Here we apply our discernment to ourselves. Knowing this tactic and capacity weak point, we preserve our emotions to ourselves, preventing any openings to be exploited.

Corruption

"You can not uncorrupt your conscience through corrupting the sense of right and wrong of any other."

The good judgment of the bullshitter is the good judgment of a cheat. All their bullshit is one massive cheat. Everything they do is in some way an try and dodge reality. One such fake logic especially is the distorted notion that if a person else is worse than you, it makes you ok. What an extremely moronic notion. One bullshitters undertake wholeheartedly as it's so exceedingly convenient for them. They want to lie to their manner to happiness, to value, to competence, to being real, to the whole lot. They even try and cheat in relation to their judgment of right and wrong!

To appease their judgment of right and wrong with their extraordinarily-better-makes-me-ok logic, they'll make every attempt to deprave the sense of right and wrong of any other. They will try to enlist you in a joint lie or cheating on some thing in your presence or, with your knowledge, making you guilty via association.

If you don't item, this may later be used to condemn you and factor out you didn't item and are therefore responsible as well. Now they "have some thing on you," and of their common sense this makes them "superior." It doesn't remember the relative degree in their transgression in comparison to yours. They will gloatingly factor out you're worse than them due to the fact you're also a big hypocrite, going into the way you "faux" to be top and high-quality, but truely you're "just like them," most effective worse due to the fact you're one of these big hypocrite.

All of that is utter bullshit, but that's what the bullshitter does. Mostly this logic isn't even expressed, but just their inner distortions on this regard are sufficient to provide them notion of their "superiority" and your "inferiority." These mis-beliefs and idiocies will happen in their demeanour and behaviour, and worse, they'll communicate their perverted attitudes of you to others. A trouble when associating with bullshitters, specially the BMN, due to the fact that we're responsible, actually through affiliation, regardless of what we do. Merely associating with a bullshitter inadvertently condones their behaviour and actions, and they'll use this reality to entangle us in their corrupt convolutions.

Discernment

"Bullshit is its personal blackhole. You cannot restore bullshit with more."

Bullshitters start with a cheat mind-set, a benefit-at-the-price-of-others perception gadget, with their insistence on indulging, no longer wanting to make any attempt, and deceiving to get what they need. Cheating, to them, represents a superiority. "Putting one over others" is specially valued.

As they pass along, as they pass similarly and in addition far from any realness, their hollowness and crappiness becomes more and more obvious to them. Refusing to well known their

154

very well stupid alternatives, they as a substitute double-down, adding ever-growing deceit to their distortions. Until everything they do is a lie, as they chase the impossibility of seeking to bullshit their way out of the jail-of-non-being they've created for themselves.

"Age-antique styles are sooner or later being discerned and exposed."

Bullshit has been around forever, for the reason that first time a person tried to gain an unethical benefit. Today however, in the data age, we're in a role we've never been in earlier than. We now have get right of entry to to pattern and records. Everything is recorded in a few way. We leave trails online, even though not performed so ourselves. Others speak approximately us, take snap shots or motion pictures people, or in other methods file what we do.

Besides this document, our get entry to to records, mainly truths, has exponentially elevated. Yes, we'd grumble on the overload of on-line bullshit, however whilst we come upon

155

real truth through recognition, insight, discernment, and know-how, we're changed. The net has expanded the spreading of these understandings notably.

We input discussions or look at them a lot more frequently than we did before the internet. All of this effects in a extra societal awareness. It's additionally led to greater mis-ideals via the ones prone to bullshit, however even they eventually run into someone, or some discussion, wherein their silly positions and ideals are shown to be exactly that, bullshit. For many that is a surprise and a rude awakening, once in a while stressful. In the overall, society is waking up. More and more as a society we're seeing and recognising bullshit for what it is, a cancer on us, and society, slowly and forever eating away. The horror of this, particularly when we're confronted with undeniable truths, accumulates until it erupts into movement.

The explosion of attention about sexual harassment and abuse, and the ensuing moves which might be being taken, is a remarkable example. Sexual harassment is excessive and harmful bullshit, in addition enabled by using the complicit bullshit of others. Perhaps we ourselves had been one of individuals who enabled, via our silence or non-action.

In the net global, we will find others, locate allies, discover individuals who will stand with us. We don't must address topics on my own anymore. We can percentage our discernment and expertise, we can percentage our studies, we can percentage our resistance and outrage, we are able to proportion our non-popularity, and thereby we will make a distinction. Times are converting, and that they're converting rapid.

"Complicity isn't an choice! Character, integrity, and ethics are critical! Appropriate-intolerance is now the order of the day! We want to step up!"

When dealing with excessive bullshit which ends up in physical or monetary damage, we will factor to their visible effect and pressure solutions. With more generalised and diffused bullshit, where the harm isn't so obvious, handling the ones negative consequences at once is greater difficult.

In this age, we've more get entry to to the effective guns of cognizance and discernment due to the fact that now we can all proportion our understandings. These discernments and understandings enter the overall consciousness whilst sufficiently shared. This is how bullshit is going down! It can't exist wherein there's attention of what it's far, of how it really works. The egregious instance of an intense bullshit-manipulator-narcissist on the world level most effective serves to hasten the social revolution that is happening.

We like to ask, "But what can I do?" The answer is clearly to act with man or woman, integrity, and ethics. If we practice those distinctly effective equipment-of-being, we can simplest recognise with regards to bullshit, we actually have to be illiberal. A new know-how to comb the sector is: suitable-intolerance!

As suitable humans, we generally tend to robotically be tolerant, believing it to always be a terrific nice, but it's no longer continually properly. To be tolerant of evil is obviously no longer true. The trouble with bullshit is it's now not obviously awful until we absolutely understand, then we see just how terrible it genuinely is. Once we see bullshit for the cancer and blight it's miles, we comprehend intolerance is known as for. Our intolerance when it comes to this sickness is absolutely appropriate.

It's hard in the context of this e book to make all of the connections we'd like. To fully apprehend, lamentably, we must delve in-depth into the information of cock-eyed psychology. Otherwise the point of interest too fast shifts to the effective replacements. Yes, those replacements are critical, and necessary, vital. But they're not the focus of this paintings immediately.

First the ones negatives need to be completely understood, to be undone and dealt with, to be unhooked from. Otherwise, we really overlay a surface on a fragile base. Without that strong expertise of primitive or confined questioning, legacy beliefs and common sense, we're inclined through our unawareness of what all is worried.

Opposite-Logic

"To figure root motive, we need to recognize the complexity at the back of simplicity."

Bullshitters disguise in the back of the simplicity of their facade, normally a facade which portrays them as being valuable in some way, despite the fact that it's handiest the small value of being "friendly." The bullshitter will visit extraordinary pains to hide themselves in a shroud of artlessness. Always they push this concept, due to the fact they're some thing however easy. As is so frequently actual of bullshitters, what they pitch is the exact opposite of what's correct, and usually that contrary applies to them. If we pay attention to what bullshitters say and do, we will see how they completely deliver themselves away via this addiction of pushing the alternative to hide their bullshit.

If they call every other a liar, it's due to the fact they're the liar. If they make a fuss about how cheating someone is, it's because they're the cheating one. If they factor out how pathetic someone else is, what a "loser" they are, it's due to the fact they're the pathetic loser. It's the reality of the bullshitter; they deliver themselves away because their simplest option to keep away from exposure is bullshit.

The extra they try to divert our interest from the awful truth of what they may be, the more they display themselves. Understanding this contrary common sense of bullshit is a effective tool-of-discernment for seeing into bullshitters.

"It is a profound act to see what is. To look at things for what they are. To be conscious and make conscious the unseen, the obscure, the covert, the intentionally hidden. To observe beliefs, convictions, habituations, motivations, and styles. Therein lies the crux. Seeing wintry weather coming is crucial for dealing with it."

Chapter 7: Disturbing Implications

Timid Criminality

"This became exciting, in that each one 40 psychopathic tendencies can pertain to someone - quite startling. However, there's one very very important component: their behaviour may be ameliorated by way of timidity, which makes a large distinction! A saving grace for some bullshitters, to some extent. But timidity may be emboldened thru associates and association."

Psychopaths are, of route, also bullshitters, however bullshitters aren't necessarily psychopaths. There's a distinction, even though there's giant overlap. All the traits of the psychopath can apply to a bullshitter, however they nevertheless aren't a psychopath. The primary reason: timidity. The bullshitter doesn't move that line into the outright illegal activity we companion with the common idea of a psychopath. (The medical definition doesn't always mean criminality.)

Usually the bullshitter is simply too scared of consequence. One of their prime motivations for bullshit is to avoid consequence. Their bullshit is precisely geared to keeping off preciseness and definitive judgements. It's chance aversion.

Bullshitters visit great pains to keep away from pronouncing or doing some thing which may be definitively "proved." They thrive at the confusion of obfuscation. Implication is their leader weapon, as they then can't directly be held responsible. Always they can revert to saying, "But that's no longer what I said! You're simply deciphering it that manner." Or similar such machinations. In this way they escape direct condemnation. Their dependancy of averting determining acts and statements continues them faraway from criminal acts in preferred.

This doesn't mean they're averse to criminal activity; they aren't. It's handiest their timidity in this regard which holds them at bay. When we completely understand the bullshitter, and the bullshit-manipulator-narcissist mainly, there are disturbing implications.

Plotting and Scheming

"The manner bullshit-manipulators 'relate' and have interaction well-knownshows a plotting and scheming rationale, a pre-determined schedule. There's not anything 'informal,' 'spontaneous,' or 'friendly' approximately these preconceived manipulations."

Let's count on a regular interaction, one that may result in some kind of dating beyond informal acquaintance. We come into touch with someone new. We recognise not anything about them. They're friendly and behave normally. We're given no indication this isn't so. They take an hobby in us, and this we love, we're flattered. Our hobby in them is now heightened. All appears properly and best.

After a few interactions we word small oddities, peculiarities, nothing in any respect critical. Trivial, minor. We placed these right down to the standard, that no longer the whole thing goes to be perfect. It's to be anticipated.

Besides, they genuinely like us, they be aware of us, are great to us. We take matters for what they appear to be.

Implications, unluckily right here, are considering that in the context of the book, this character is probably going to become a bullshit-manipulator-narcissist. The implication is we need to anticipate and potentially examine all people as a capability BMN. This honestly doesn't must be so. We don't have to cross round suspecting all and sundry we meet. All we need to be privy to, is the possibility. That's enough typically.

If we add an knowledge and a full designated observe simply one BMN, after that we'll recognize the clues without problems. Once we recognise, it's apparent. The obvious is usually so after we end up aware. Here lies the value of this e-book, to make recognising a bullshitter obvious.

"Corrupt desires and motivations beginning corrupt strategies."

In our newly shaped courting, on account that we now recognise about bullshitters, when you consider that we are able to now recognize them and understand their underlying common sense, we begin to see things otherwise. Their motivations and intents show. We see after they're being satisfactory to us, their goal isn't really to make us glad, but it's all about how it makes them appearance. We see how they jockey for popularity, even status relative to us. We see their assumptions, how they take as a right they're "advanced" and other such nonsense. We see how they have an agenda. Once we be aware those agendas, their bullshit is simple to realize.

Most critical, we ask, "What's their cause here?" Just asking this query makes all of the distinction. Just asking reveals that rationale. Or sufficient to make it clear their purpose is all approximately them, all about pretence, all approximately bullshit.

We're targeted right here on implication. Once we see this new "friend" is all about self-merchandising, the usage of, pretending, manipulating, and how they are only rationale on the rubbish of the bullshitter, we see any actual relationship is an impossibility. Always, if we appearance a piece in addition with such individuals, we end up on the implications of crappy intent.

Deliberate Schemes

"When the intention is indulgence, it exhibits a corrupt mind-set."

Once we've known a bullshitter, usually the most expedient course of movement is to terminate all interactions and any relationship. In the pursuits of our learning and awareness, it's maximum beneficial to dangle on for just a bit to have a look at the behaviour. Especially to study the results. Until we honestly see for ourselves, implications are simply theoretical. Once we see them play out, once we see that fact come about, then we understand, and we provide ourselves an opportunity to expand trust in our perceptions and understandings.

Watching a bullshitter in movement once we understand what they're as much as famous disturbing implications. We get to look how the whole thing they do is a deliberate scheme. We see how they usually have their time table of self first, their schedule of creating an image, of getting something for nothing, their schedule of dominance, and all the different pathetic intents they have got.

"Bullshitters are perpetual and persistent opportunists jumping at each glimmer of hazard out of necessity, as their loss of ability and abilities, their reliance on bullshit, and as a consequence their insecurity forces this incessant greed for unearned praise."

The worrying element is to see how planned it all is, how ever-gift those motivations, agendas and intents are. How they recognize they're bullshitting. How they recognise they're false and phoney. How crappy and squirrelly and unethical they are. Yet they do what they do besides. Yet they intentionally bullshit and control besides. This is the annoying component. That conscious deliberation. It's difficult to trust or comprehend with out seeing it for oneself.

Fortunately, we don't have to get into a relationship or interaction with a bullshitter to examine this. There are plenty possibilities on TV or on-line to have a look at this. Just being conscious that in relation to bullshit, there are stressful implications is enough to enable our bullshit radar.

Shared Responsibility

"Trying to emotionally and energetically bully and coerce others into respecting you is astonishingly preposterous! And folks that allow and buy into it are themselves ludicrous - they keep the antique system! They aid and keep a global-view that's unethical!"

Disturbing implications don't only practice to the bullshitter and the BMN; they may practice to us as properly. For example, if we purchase into hierarchy and use the mechanisms of superiority, even though handiest a touch bit, and assume it's okay while we do it, but no longer ok when others do it to us, the consequences for us aren't quite. It works both approaches. Even if we do "most effective a little," the annoying implications are we help maintain a bullshit gadget, we're complicit and culpable in that corruption. When the BMN bullies and abuses a person else in that gadget, we're, by using implication, also partly responsible.

Bullshit Posse

"When a bullshitter not feels the want to bullshit, once they experience they are able to break out with their indulgences with no need the quilt of pretence, that's when they step absolutely into the world of abuse."

Bullshitter-manipulator-narcissists particularly are emboldened with the aid of aid. The greater their bullshit is pandered to, the greater their ego and conceitedness is supported via sycophants and toadies, the extra they arrive to consider their personal delusion and the more emboldened they get. Those feeding this beast refuse to stand the bad implications concerned until it's too past due, and that they emerge as acutely aware about those devastating implications as the beast devours them. Most bad.

Whenever encountering a bullshitter or a BMN with their own aid institution, be ultra wary. That limit of timidity usually in play is not a safety. These bullshitters can be, or can end up, capable of something. It's here they begin to cross over into outright criminal activity and emerge as even greater risky.

The implications of this degree are they now not really want the bullshit. They have what they crave, they're dominant, they're being flattered, they're receiving all the attention, and once they realize they could bully and dominate with abandon, they permit go of the need for the bullshit and allow their ugly selves to flourish. It's at this degree wherein gaslighting to control and "personal" turns into an choice. Disturbing implications certainly.

Impossible Relationships

"The comparative-mindset and the lack of self-honesty limits surely referring to."

If we're possibly tempted to go into a dating with a bullshitter, we but want keep in mind one traumatic implication: bullshitters are incapable of having a actual courting. It's simply no longer viable. When the whole lot of someone's cause is to "promote" a fake self, how can they be in a actual dating? The relationship can be with a phantom; how is it feasible? Not most effective is this a traumatic implication, however the bullshitter is targeted only on themselves and getting out of the family members just what benefits them. They need it all. How can that paintings? It can't. Not for us besides. Implications are effective, if we don't shrink back from those that are disturbing.

"'Blackholes' are a one-way deal unto themselves. There's no manner to really 'keep' a blackhole. Love is mild, and the more that's added, the greater is absorbed, it's an impossibility. Any giving to a blackhole best provides to it. The handiest course of action is to avoid it totally, to be out of its have an impact on completely, and simply allow it do what blackholes do. They implode sooner or later, if now not fed. That's their manner, and that's what they choose. That grabbing and grabbing, that relentless taking, that's the pleasure of the blackhole."

It's worth repeating: implications are effective equipment, if we don't steer away from those which might be worrying.

An rationale of this e-book is to change social recognition by way of making it clean how critical and devastating bullshit is. Not a easy problem. For instance, certain perspectives on victims, along with, "the victim is likewise guilty" or "the victim need to bear some obligation." There are many that accept as true with some version of this.

If a person is captured by slavers, it is out in their fingers. A psychology can be similarly captured. Something the overall public don't recognize. BMNs are slavers like that. They deliberately go about enslaving some other's psychology and being. Typically their sufferers have little choice. There are many disturbing implications with regards to how bullshit performs out.

Most true humans make the effort to look to more, to look past the crapola to extra, to sensibility or spirituality. They're aware about the crappy aspect of human beings, and the depths of it. In widespread, with most human beings, they're no longer aware about the whole depths of positive psychologies. Unfortunately, this reasons issues and has implications.

We just should examine society's ordinary attitude and mindset to all the aspects of bullshit to peer the superficial perspective of bullshit. Bullshit is "BS" to most. It's this poo-pooing of bullshit as a minor trouble which permits the bullshitters, and which ends up in BMNs, to their extremes, their abuse, and them getting away with it. All because of inadvertent complicity and accidental condoning, at some point of lack of full cognizance of the severity of the difficulty. It without a doubt is a huge deal.

"The preposterous, the bogus, the fake, the phoney, the frauds, - exist, yet are unreal."

Another example of the deeper trouble is the general assumed misogyny certainly taken for granted by means of maximum guys. For instance, they subscribe to hierarchy in some way to extremely various stages, but generally it's there.

Thing is, for most of them, women aren't protected in that hierarchy. They're not even conscious of this taken for granted misogyny. It's great bullshit. One massive cause why the focus of this book must be tight. It's to make us, as a society, aware of the implications and results of those small bullshits, like that assumed inadvertent misogyny and the way it ends up having intense and enormous results.

A massive hassle is the complexity of bullshit. It's not neat and tidy and linear. It's a large sphere of complexity with many aspects to it all. When that complete sphere is thought and understood, dealing with bullshit is tons simplified. But difficult to communicate.

The problem of bullshit is a specific one. To get out from it, we first should immerse into it to recognize its complete complexity. Once we apprehend, the direction for managing it and lowering it in society as an entire is plain. When we understand the excessive outcomes of what seems benign and trivial, the overpowering majority people can't partake in those small reputedly insignificant moves of transgression or complicity while we know what they lead to. Most people do have moral sense and ethics, but thru lack-of-awareness these are lamentably no longer always activated.

"When we absolutely apprehend the severity of a scenario, we will not overlook or forget about."

Ethical Complications

Repeated Transgressing

"These bullshit-manipulators are humans in our every day lives, in our community, and accessible in our global. They're there for themselves and their self-promotion. They 'play' anybody. Their con is always on. Some want to think themselves exempt, being pretty pleasant with the truth that so long as they're now not being preyed on, it's alright. How does that make it k?"

The no-fault logic, or forgiveness philosophy, is one many love, aspire to, and spot notable value in. However, it best works if all participants have integrity. For the fast-reduce mentality, which is primary to the BMN, this is a incredible possibility to take advantage of, manage, abuse, and take from those who join this best or comparable. They rub their fingers with glee at the possibility of transgressing, then clearly pronouncing "sorry" and, once forgiven, and all is reset, to then repeat the transgression. They will try this again and again again, as long as they're allowed to get away with this thoroughly unscrupulous, unethical, and shitty behaviour.

Good humans discover it hard to agree with or realise a person can be so low and dastardly, and nicely, evil, when it comes to such behaviour, but if we're to be sincere and practice our integrity to all of life, we should well known this sad reality exists.

Animal Psychology

"The onus is on us to deal with the inconvenient stress of the emotional and active manipulations of the squirrelly, smarmy, conscienceless creatures in our midst, be they 'lover', 'pal', father, brother, sister, mother, colleague or neighbour."

We have to be careful in assuming all who look like humans are, in truth, generally or in general human. Sometimes, even though they may be human their behaviour comes from an animal-like psychology.

An instance of this mindset: a pleasing woman notices raccoons scavenging for meals in her trash can. She feels sorry for them and leaves some food out. At first the raccoons are cautious, worried of the human. Soon they recognise the pleasant woman will no longer, certainly can not, hurt nor damage them. The nice female is taken in by means of their "friendliness," permitting them into her domestic. The raccoons take advantage, and the exceptional girl forgives them, not able to assign responsibility or take negative seeming measures. She doesn't want to have interaction in "negativity' or unpleasantness. Pretty quickly the raccoons realise this and end up taking over her home, pushing the nice female out. Turning competitive towards her as she attempts to get at her own food for herself.

Sadly, many a properly-which means charity employee has had their coronary heart, beliefs, and psychologies crushed via simply such instances, except, of path, with humans. Niceness to a few is the same as weak spot, and is simplest to be exploited and taken gain of.

Realistic Options

"There's no equality in chicken-land."

Admirable beliefs are admirable, however most effective in the event that they're tempered with sensibility and sensible applicability, and specially, appropriateness. Applying an interactive philosophy and psychology meant for ethical people with integrity, to the unethical or those with primitive mindsets is foolish and inappropriate. We need to hold this in mind with regards to coping with some people. Yes, they do have the capability for trade, and positivity, however until such capacity is realised, we have to act and behave in accordance to what is, not according to what we wish for or hope for.

With that being stated, if we've got the energy, time, and condition, we can be instrumental in supplying possibility for others to behave and behave in ways completely a-typical to them. We can even lead them, and in a wonderful manner even guide their willingness to choose from more nice alternatives of behaviour. A guidance towards an consciousness of greater picks. This is a behaviour which calls for some talent and focus of no longer-so-advantageous psychology, not to say a diploma of independence-of-being and cognizance. But is honestly viable and practicable.

"It is incumbent on us to now not condone the squirrelly among us. - If we've inadvertently achieved so by way of being naive, trusting, and believing their lies, the lesson is to order one's support until we're positive, and thereby not allowing the morally defunct among us through untimely moves."

Unfortunately, the demands and pressures of our truth, the urgencies of condition, necessitate we use whatever tool is at our disposal. Usually, the only is easy avoidance. But to keep away from we should first realize, and it's to this stop a good deal of this ebook is geared.

"If we can see trouble before it sees us, getting out of the manner is straightforward."

Chaos-Profiteers

Contamination and Confusion

"Bullshit-manipulators don't simply contaminate an environment; they smash them. They're parasites who bring down the host, whoever and whatever that might be.

Sowing chaos and 'exhilaration' to disrupt and capture opportunity for themselves."

Every minute, each 2d, of the BMN's lifestyles is full of the stress of pretence. They're below danger of exposure with each single utterance and behavior. A constant pressure which manifests in diverse approaches, normally re-diverted negativity on those luckless sufficient to be deemed unworthy of the want to electrify, allure, flatter, or whose interest would not count number.

This stress in no way relents, there's by no means any respite. They love chaos, for this is the only time not anything subjects. In chaos they are able to do something, be whatever, and it doesn't depend. In chaos they may be unfettered and unrestrained, permitting their every indulgence to run wild. Chaos hence represents a release from that ever-present hazard of exposure.

"Bullshit-manipulators love confusion due to the fact they can take rate and escape with their unsavoury objectives. There's a manic feel approximately getting a leg-up during chaos. The preference for chaos lets in the unscrupulous to sense like they're 'leaders' who can 'do what they need,' dominating others and implementing otherwise untenable activities and intents. Chaos 'legitimises' bullshit. Who can tell bullshit from reality all through chaos? It for that reason will become easy and simpler to seem rather 'higher.'"

Chaos represents large possibility to the BMN. They crave being "leaders" and "instructors," even authorities and such like, however they seldom own the needful abilities or want to make the precise efforts to justify being such human beings. Also, being in such positions magnifies ability scrutiny, and consequently possible publicity. A conundrum and capture-22 for the BMN. In instances of chaos, none of that subjects. They recognise when the whole lot is falling aside, all people can be a "leader."

The BMN sees chaos as a brilliant commencing, as in environments of disruption. It's whoever seizes the lead who gets the lead. Qualifications, history, reputation, man or woman aren't an issue, as there normally isn't always time or scenario to check and confirm. First in receives the plum. Mostly in occasions of mayhem, human beings are just too satisfied a person, each person, is taking rate and taking duty. Thus the BMN grabs this chance. They can soar in, bullshit flying, and be obtained with open fingers.

Control

"Bullshitters like to purpose emotional chaos, which they then take benefit of."

www.ingramcontent.com/pod-product-compliance
Lightning Source LLC
Chambersburg PA
CBHW071331120626
46546CB00002B/518